# THE

# LIBERATION

# OF THE

# AFRICAN

# AMERICAN

# Contents

# Introduction

I grew up in a traditional African American family, which attended a Baptist church, and I also attended a desegregated school system in the state of Georgia. Over time, I had learned to accept the African American experience at face value and just cope with the pain and insecurities associated with being born black in America. As a young adult I joined the United States Marine Corp Reserves, had acquired a state job in addition to attending college; I felt like my life was heading in the right direction because I had learned to repress my pain. But as months turned to years and years turned to decades, I began to slowly change. I would see on television how police brutality was still an issue for the African American race and how so many continued to struggle in life. This drove me to question my very purpose for existence on this planet, and no one could answer such a question except me. I then decided I had to find myself, I began to read spiritual books and meditate daily. After about five years of daily meditation and having read several books my perception began to change. It was as though I could see the true reasons behind certain events and no longer was able to accept the worldly reasons for events as truth. I no longer saw slavery as just slavery, but I could see the movement of Creation associated with slavery. I no longer saw segregation as depicted in school, I could see the truth behind it. These truths are there in the universal mind for all of us to understand if we only silence the carnal mind.

The content of this book comes from a silent mind that through meditation and the elimination of the self has opened the third eye and the crown chakras and is now in tune with the universal mind. This book is a look at the true nature of the African American race and why Creation has chosen to create us. We must understand that if we try to understand God with the carnal mind, we become trapped in the illusion. It is only when our minds are silent can we hear the words of the Father and only then will we truly understand. Upon becoming open to the universal mind it was then I could look back at all of the pain and emotional stress I had been harboring because I was a black in American and realized it was all because I lacked the understanding needed to see the truth. I had sought knowledge about my reality from the outer world and had not looked inside of myself for the truth that every human has within himself. We must understand we cannot find truth in the outer realms of reality. The truth is within us and it is only when we gain control of our beliefs, thoughts, and words can we understand these truths. This book should be read as many times as needed to gain the necessary understanding to free your mind from the chains that have been placed on it since you were able to falsely understand the world around you. As an African American, you have two choices; you can realize these chains exist and strive to free yourself from these chains or you can remain a host to a parasite that will daily drain your life force. If you choose to remain a host then you will pass this parasite which is the misinterpretation of the African American experience to your next generation. We have an opportunity to change this paradigm through the understanding of truth. And it is in accepting these truths, which yield a change of our core beliefs about our past experiences we can then become free from bondage. But one thing we must all realize, it is only through the collective effort of our race to embrace fully these new truths can we assist Creation in fostering in these changes and then create a beautiful world for our African American children.

# Chapter 1

# Slavery and its Effects

The history of African-American slavery is mostly taught to our youth as just a past event that the ancestors of African Americans endured. No one teaches our children or even the adults about the mental scars that are still present in the psyche of all African Americans. Therefore, lack of teaching affects our everyday interaction with each other and other races. Nor are we taught to look deep within ourselves and understand the evolution of the African American race. One destructive scar that still exists from slavery is the lack of trust we have for each other. The truth is, not all our ancestors were captured by Europeans; some sold into slavery by other Africans. The act of selling your fellow African to another race to enslave almost undeniable states that there were already issues before the Caucasians landed on the continent. This single act of selling your own race has facilitated in four generations of African American the feeling that your own race is not to be trusted. It would seem more understandable that due to the horrible experiences of slavery the race would have united against one common foe, but the distrust was woven too deep in the psyche of the African American and this alone made unity impossible. And this ideology of not trusting is currently still affecting black interaction as a whole. A staggering 90.1% of all blacks murdered in America are murdered by other blacks. So then I ask how a race can reach its full potential without being able to trust one another. It will not reach its' full potential. A football team wins the super bowl only when every player on the team understands his role in relation to the common goal, and trust is a cultural attribute, not an established rule. In the black communities, trust is neither a cultural attribute nor a rule it is simply absent. The opposite of trust is distrust which simply means, to have no confidence in; doubt or suspect. Therefore the black community has no confidence in or doubts its own people, abilities, and business relations. This unwillingness to trust each other keeps blacks from establishing successful businesses in the black community due to a lack of support from the community it serves. When I was younger, I knew an African American business owner name Mr. Watson, who owned a loan company in a small town. I oftentimes heard other African Americans who lived in that community saying I am going to take my business to the white man because I know he will give me a better deal. They could not see the importance of supporting businesses owned by their own race, and how it helps the community. These same people oftentimes ended up unable to repay the loans and ended up losing property or their wages being garnished. Meanwhile, a large amount of Mr. Watson's business had become white customers because in truth Mr. Watson offered the best interest rate on the loans. But the question I had to ask myself at an early age was why the African Americans in that community did not give Mr. Watson a chance. Instead, they decided not to engage in business with him because of an assumption or were it something deeper in their subconscious mind. Collectively, we must understand that we lost trust in each other because of slavery and this distrust still thrives in the subconscious mind of every African American today. When we choose not to support another African American's business in our community, we are acting unknowingly from a state of mind that derives from what our ancestors endured during slavery. When we choose to trust in another race for products that our own race offers we are acting from a plantation state of mind. This plantation state of mind is defined as a state of mind which an entire race of people believe at a subconscious level that they must depend on another race to provide the basic essentials for life and these necessities cannot be provided by their own race. These essentials are food, water, clothes and shelter, which all came from the white slave masters. Therefore, in this plantation state of mind, we cannot fathom being able to receive products from a business owner of the same race as ours. We tend to see his products as inferior or think his prices are too high. In some cases, we feel we are equal to the White community when we are able to buy our products from the white-owned business. But this plantation mindset is not limited to the support of white business instead of black businesses it seems to be present with all other races also. I once knew a young lady by the name of Alisha who decided to open a hair store that sold black hair products. The location of her new business venture was directly across the street from an Asian owned hair store that also sold primarily black hair products. Needless to say, I was interested in how the African American community would react. For the past eight years, they had supported the Asian owned hair store, therefore, putting money in the Asian community, would this paradigm change with the opening of an African American owned hair store? After about a month of operation, my question was answered. I would ride by and see one or two cars at Alisha's hair store and the Asian own hair store would be packed with customers purchasing hair products for the weekend. So I decided to ask one of the young ladies exiting the Asian owned hair store why didn't she give her business to the black-owned stores and she stated, "Alisha probably doesn't have anything I want in there." This was a clear representation of the plantation mindset that African Americans possess subconsciously that causes our businesses to fail and our lack of trust to continue to grow. This young lady and probably many others assumed they would not be satisfied with the products that the black-owned hair store had to offer, therefore didn't give Alisha an opportunity to serve them. Unfortunately, after attempting to get business from the African American community and failing Alisha closed her doors after being open for only six months. Without trusting in each other there can be no true growth. If Alisha's hair store would have been successful in the community she could have given jobs back to the community. But so many of us cannot see the importance of investing in our own communities, creating our own jobs and being self sufficient. Therefore we rely on some other race to invest in our communities, create businesses and jobs for our people. Only 6% of black money goes back into the black community and in the Jewish community money changes hand 18 times before leaving their community. Can you see the differences in the mentality of the races? And when we fail to see the importance of becoming self sufficient we are still on the plantation, but only on the modern day model of a plantation.

If we closely examine the slavery plantations, we can see that slaves were forced to create a world inside of the world. This simply means the world as they knew it was not a true representation of the world, but one that was forced on them by their slave masters. We also must understand that there were free blacks in the Northern states who had an opportunity to experience the world and not an illusion forced on them by being enslaved. And if we examine some of our inner-city ghettos today we can see that plantations continue to exit. Only instead of being forced to create a world inside of the world by the slave owners, we are forced to do so by our government and laws. And these illusionary plantations that exit we tend to call them our hoods, the projects, or the ghetto. Many of the African American population have become truly free and are able to experience the world and are no longer attached to the plantation, but a large portion of the African American population unknowingly are living on modern day plantations. On these modern day plantations, they are given all of the basic necessities to help them remain as a loyal member of the plantation. There are alcohol stores on every corner, drugs of all kinds being sold on every corner, low rent, and even guns brought in to maintain a murder rate. These modern day plantations are heavenly patrolled by police just as the plantations during slavery were patrolled. In other words, the people living in the inner city are still contained just as their ancestors were in slavery. During slavery, our ancestors had to obtain freedom to experience the world and today we have to obtain money to experience the world. In the eyes of some of the African Americans today and during slavery, it was easier to live in a self-created world than to pay the price to experience the true world, therefore they embrace the plantation mindset. This plantation mindset embodies all of the morals and beliefs that the slaves created that still exist in the collective consciousness of African Americans. The collective consciousness of a race consists of shared internal beliefs, ideas, and moral attitudes that operate as the governing forces of how that race perceives and experiences the physical world. One of the most destructive attributes passed down over generations by slaves that still lives in the subconscious minds of African Americans is the crabs in a barrel mentality. The basis of this quote is that when crabs are in a bucket or barrel every time one tries to reach the top of the barrel another crab pulls him down. This translated into human interactions is simply having the mentality, if I can't have it, neither can you. This mentality that plagues the African American community derived from the house slaves. These slaves worked in the house and were not subject to the harsh treatment that the field slaves had to endure. These slaves were often envied by the field slaves because they were perceived to be closer to the slave masters. The field slaves felt that the more impressed slave masters were with the performance of a slave or the closer one could become to the slave master, the better off life on the plantation would be. This fostered in our subconscious minds the energy of jealousy towards our brothers and sisters. This illusion of somehow having it better than another slave destroyed the element of loyalty between slaves, therefore creating the crabs in the barrel mentality that plagues us today. This mentality attacks our communities at the family level and at the friendship level. Both our friends and family members' opinions have an influence on most of our decisions and when we are attacked at this level, we tend to fall back into the barrel with all the other crabs. In other words, we tend to believe those we feel care about our futures and we alter our future plans based on their opinions. I once knew a teenager named Justin, who lived in the inner city of Atlanta. Justin was only twelve years of age and was a part of the second generation of his family to live in poverty and the ghetto. This teenager wanted to change this paradigm and move out of this world within a world and experience life, but the energies of the ghetto had other plans. Justin was an honor roll student and wanted to go to college and become a doctor, but his friends from the ghetto whom he had grown up with had a different future in mind. The future that they had in mind would not remove them from the ghetto which seems to have the attributes of a modern plantation, but keep them deeply entrenched in the ghetto. The future they envisioned involved joining a gang and selling drugs to make a living. They felt they could become prosperous like some of the older drug dealers on the street corners, that they could have new cars and nice clothes. And when Justin told them about what he aspired to do, they all began to laugh and stated, you, trying to get out of the hood, nobody leaves the hood. We are about to join this gang next week so we can make some real money, you had better join us or be left out. Day by day, this decision weighed heavily on Justin's mind until he too could not imagine himself getting off the plantation or rather the ghetto. The other crabs had pulled him back into the barrel just as he was planning his escape. After days of pondering, he decided to join the gang and live the only prosperous life he truly knew. That Friday evening along with his friends Justin was headed to be sworn into the gang at the age of twelve. His friends could not imagine any other world, but as Justin walked with his friends his imagination kept drifting back to the white coat of a doctor. In that moment Justin realized that without a dream you lose yourself in the illusion and he turned to his friends and said, "I am not joining a gang that is not the life I envisioned for myself." "One day I will become a doctor and I will leave this hood." His friends all laughed and continue to walk saying, "he will be back no one gets out of the hood." You see at the age of twelve Justin realized the importance of imagination and how striving to fulfill your dream takes you away from becoming a product of your environment. His friends had subconsciously decided to remain loyal patrons of the plantation now being the ghetto because they lack the ability to imagine a different life for themselves. And because they couldn't imagine leaving the hood and they didn't want any better for Justin. Justin continued to follow his dream and became a doctor and his friends were in and out of prison and confined to the plantation (ghetto) because of a lack of a dream. We as a people have to overcome this crabs in a barrel mentality that derived from slavery, and get off of the plantations. We can do this simply by having a dream and pursuing that dream with all our hearts. And when we see our brothers and sisters pursuing their dreams we must support them and not be jealous or make negative comments. When you do this you must see yourself as the crab and immediately begin to change. Only by dreaming and having support from our friends and family can we begin to see the world as it truly is and not live as our ancestors did, in a forced self made world. When we choose to live in this illusion we subconsciously choose to keep the plantation thriving, but as we choose to dream and we leave the plantation we are subconsciously releasing negative energy that has kept so many of us confined for generations. We as a people must discover true freedom.

Secondly, there is very little discussed in American history about the conditions of the slave ships and what actually facilitated our loss of identity. Prior to boarding slave ships located on the West coast of Africa, many slaves were made to kneel before the cross and accept Christianity as their new religion. This was the beginning of the shift in who we were as a people to what we are now. An entire race of people cannot change what we believe without becoming confused and lost which is where we are now. In conforming to be like another race of people you lose yourself in their dreams because now you only dream to be like them. The slaves were shackled and the slave ships were overcrowded, therefore restricting the movement and freedom of an individual. The bellies of the ships were oftentimes hot, dark, and filled with moans and cries.

These were moans of pain and cries for the  loved ones they had been separated from. These cries were from mothers, fathers, and children. Can you imagine children in the belly of a ship separated from the parent who has protected them their entire little lives and now subject to torment? Often time's slaves were also given temporary names and forced to respond to these new names, therefore, stripping them of the heritage. The floor of the lower deck was usually covered with excrement, urine, mucous, and vomit. Most slave ships only had a few buckets the slaves used for urine and excrement. And because slaves were shackled and suffered bruises trying to get to the buckets most preferred relieve waste in their personal space. The human mind cannot even begin to imagine the smell that slaves had to endure in the bellies of slave ships. Most trips to America took only a couple of months, but it seemed like years to slaves. Slaves received minimal exercise and were washed very few times during their voyages. Therefore slaves were diseased due to conditions, broken people due to shackles and dehumanizing conditions. Some slaves often times tried to commit suicide by starvation or jumping into the Atlantic Ocean. Although most of these attempts were met with resistance by the slave traders, some slaves were successful and some died due to the conditions. It was discussed in several slave ship journals that sharks over time became familiar with the slave trade routes and would no longer hunt in the ocean. They would follow the slave ships and consume the dead bodies of slaves being tossed into the ocean. Again, it is difficult to comprehend the pain of seeing your loved one being thrown into the ocean and devoured by sharks. It is human nature to want to bury a family member in a sacred place and not in the ocean. But even in these moments of pain, we as African Americans must understand that there were greater forces at work than just the dumping of our dead ancestors' bodies in the ocean. What was actually happening was the transmutation of a race by eliminating the weaker genes and only allowing the stronger genes to reach the new world. In other words, now Creation was beginning, therefore yielding a new race that had superior physical and mental endurance. We must also understand that for such a process to happen our race had to be stripped of all we held dear to us. In sociology, the process our ancestors endured is called the mortification of self. This process occurs when one is stripped of their old selves and must learn to live in a new environment under entirely new rules. This process also includes the separation from family, friends, and norms. This initial process of mortification of self which occurred in our ancestor during the time trapped on slave ships facilitated the actual beginning of our race. All of these dehumanizing conditions, being stripped of our names, religion, and heritage gradually facilitated the shift from what we were before slavery to who we are now. This has to be accepted as the true origin of African American history for our growth to begin. Our ancestors were forced to accept being inferior and to accept whatever punishment came to them during these slave voyages, and in so many ways this is still our mindset as a race. This mindset continues to exist because we fail to comprehend that the slave ships were the catalyst for the beginning of a race that is superior to all other races on the planet, and we continue to wonder as a whole who we really are? This wondering about who we truly are eats at the souls of every African American because we want to have a history other than slavery. And not wanting to accept slavery and the slave ships as the origin of the African American race causes us to research history and take DNA test all to dispute our true origin. When we denounce slavery as our origin, we also tell the universe that we denounce the power associated with being the strongest race. We must look deep within our being to truly understand that there were greater forces at work during slavery that our ancestors were hand-picked by the universe to endure the pain associated with slavery. And the outcome of slavery is a level of mental and physical endurance not known to man. To have African American blood pumping in your veins is to be a part of the newly created race that possesses the wit of the Caucasians and the physical attributes of an African. To truly be capable of grasping this concept we must look at where the Europeans were on their evolutionary timetable during the time of the great kingdoms of Egypt. While the Egyptians were writing and creating Geometry and other mathematics the Europeans was still an uncivilized race with no written language. But as Europeans scholars begin to learn and interact with the Egyptian they begin to receive their knowledge and their evolution into who they are today had begun. This is how evolution works and when we understand this we will see that we are merely evolving as all races on this planet has. We are a fairly new creation with unlimited potential and we have the forces of the universe behind us. And when we understand what the universe has given us, then and only we will take our rightful place in the physical world. We have one obstacle to hurdle and that is because of slavery, we feel we are a great deal less than what we truly are. We must realize the power that slavery instilled within us and move forward. We must accept that we are a blank piece of paper created by the universe and begin to write our own history and what we want our race to be. We must realize we are no longer on the slave ship and that the shackles are gone and we are free to imagine and create. We must understand that we were never inferior, but only in a state of learning and becoming. And that in these states there are always pain and suffering, but upon the completion of these states, our light will finally shine upon the world. But one must wonder how can we remove the misunderstandings of the past which are present in the subconscious minds of African Americans and enter the bright future that awaits us?

In history, we are often taught just a slight overview of what the slaves had to endure once they made it to the New World called America, but never about how it affects us as a race today. In most cases, slaves were often with family members on the voyage to the New

World, which made it easier to bare the dehumanizing conditions they were in. All humans have a longing for a family or what is called a sense of belonging and when this desire is fulfilled in most situations a human can find some comfort. But in most cases when the slaves reached America, they were auctioned off to new masters and families were often separated. That means mother from children, husband from wife and so on and so forth. This separation from everything our ancestors loved and cherished created the mindset of a servant because there was nothing to live for but hope. Nothing the slave masters forced them to endure while on those plantations was more painful than the loss of their sons and daughters. This pain is what caused our people to cope with the everyday struggles of slavery and not commit mass suicides because they were already dead inside.  The slaves that built this country were mere hollow souls or just shells of men because the pain had taken away everything that embodies a thriving human existence. In these situations a man does not fear a hanging, lashes, or any other bodily pain, he only waits for the day that death dawns his doorstep or to be finally reunited with those he cherished. This state of being was the state that carried the first generations of slaves through this turmoil and ushered in a second generation who were born into slavery and didn't share their pain but learned to behave as their parents did. Even though on very few plantations were families separated and children being sold from their mothers and fathers rare, this learned behavior continued to survive. Most slave owners preferred breeding their slaves to ensure that their next generation of slaves would be stronger of better quality than past generations. And although the second generation couldn't even begin to comprehend such pain endured by the first, through learned behavior they adopted, the servant mentality without even knowing its true origin. And because the African-American race has not been taught the origin of this mentality or is even aware that this mentality dwells within our communities we continue to conduct ourselves as loyal servants and not as leaders. But if we are able to again look deep into our being, we will see that something greater was transpiring than just slaves being servants. A student has to be subservient to his teacher for learning to take place and slaves had to be subservient to their slave masters to learn and to fulfill the universal plan for the African American race. The Universal God knew that the only way this newly evolved race will learn from another race is that it is forced to do so. This need to force the slaves to learn is the true reason for the enslavement of our ancestors. It was through this restriction of freedom that our ancestors were able to truly learn the Europeans. For over four hundred years, our ancestors watched every move of their slave masters, learning what drove the Caucasians. And over time, we had gained such a high level of wit and cunning that we were able to assist in the fighting of the civil war and gaining our freedom. This gaining of freedom was not a coincident but a part of a universal plan that is still unfolding. And also after those four hundred years, we learned to coexist with the Caucasians and we even eventually gained equal rights under the constitution. We must begin to embrace the reason for this servant mentality and its' origin, and when we embrace this energy with understanding it loses its power over us. This simply means we become free and no longer see ourselves and our ancestors as slaves, instead we understand slavery was an illusion of a greater coming. It was simply Creation's way of hiding a newly evolved race from other races on the planet. We must begin to remove this generational learned behavior of being a servant, which was misunderstood by the masses and replace it with the truth. We must realize our self-worth and the journey that the African American race is on, and the only way to do this is to release ourselves from the falsehood of the servant mentality that plagues us today. Our misunderstanding of the servant mentality causes our communities to think we are inferior and when we collectively think this way that is what our communities become. Therefore, it is of the utmost importance that the African American communities collectively understand the true reason behind such a mentality, and utilize it to spark a new level of growth for the race.

Next, we must collectively begin to understand the effect of slavery on the family structure of the African-American race. Slavery was the great destroyer of our family structure and continues to plague our race today without us being consciously aware. A slave could be in his house with his family and the slave master could walk in and force his wife to have sex while he and his children watched. The slave could only watch while the slave master had his way with his screaming wife. Also, a married male and female slave could have a baby and on several accounts, the slave master would take the child or even kill the child in front of the mother and father. And even more destructive to the slave family on several accounts a homosexual slave master would even rape a male slave in front of his wife, family, and other slaves. In this situation, the wife was forced to watch her screaming husband be beaten and raped. The slave masters also would take the wife and beat her while her husband, children, and other family members watched. In all the situations above the power to protect all that is sacred to a human being was lost and still seems to be lost today. Every act above removed power from the male head in the families of African slaves and created a woman who felt she must be strong even stronger than her husband. It created a woman who felt she could not trust her husband to be there to take care of her and the kids and she must always be prepared for the male to leave. This fear that her male counterpart would leave helped create a woman that felt she needed no man. These feelings were passed down from generation to generation and now we are still dealing with the mothers of our race not trusting the fathers of our race and it clearly stems from slavery. These situations also created a black male that has a deep-rooted sense that he doesn't possess the qualities to maintain a family and runs from the responsibility. This is because throughout slavery the aspect of the family was taken from most male slaves on many occasions, and this pain created in the male slaves and a need to be removed from this pain. Therefore, male slaves would not truly love to avoid the pain of separation from those they love, or would simply leave. This feeling was passed down through the generations and emerged into the black males sleeping with our women, but not staying around to invest in the future of our children. This became what is known as the player mentality. This mentality clearly evolved from fear of separation. We may not understand these concepts as a race, but the government understands what occurred through slavery and how important a sound family structure is to the evolution of a race. This is why section eight housing was created, to keep the black family from reuniting. The government placed low-income families in housing, but the father couldn't stay in the household, thus eliminating the backbone of the African American family. Also, the creation of child support also helps to destroy the black family. If you stay in public housing, we will give you welfare, food stamps, and in exchange we will place the male on child support. And if he fails to make payments, we will place him in jail. Can we not see that our government understands what happened in slavery? I graduated high school with an African American couple who had been dating sporadically the entire time in high school. Janice and Matthew were their names. They both were not loyal to their relationship and would oftentimes cheat on each other. This behavior continued for about two years after graduating high school until Janice became pregnant. Now the couple was faced with the decision whether to come together and be responsible parents or to continue their irresponsible behaviors. Matthew decided to continue his lifestyle in modern terms being a player and not act as a responsible adult with a baby on the way. He continues to have interment relationships with other women and continues to be reckless with his time and money. He was not trying to prepare for the birth of his child and Janice continued to stay with her parents while working at Burger King. Janice had no health insurance, therefore being forced to receive Medicaid to ensure she could be seen by a doctor and not create issues for her unborn child during her pregnancy. During her sixth month of her pregnancy, Janice decided to move into a low-income apartment because she didn't want her child to become a burden to her parents. And upon moving into her apartment she received food stamps and several other sources of government assistance, but the end result was that Matthew would have to pay child support and could not live in the household with his son. Upon the child's birth, Matthew was placed on child support which he could not pay because he was unemployed. The newborn baby was provided with a place to stay, milk, food, and healthcare by the government and Matthew was placed in jail for missing child support payments. So, let us closely examine the situation between Janice and Matthew. The newborn needed things which the government provided, however, in exchange for Matthew's freedom. Now, this is in no way advocating not trying to support your children, but due to the government stepping in both mother and father now owed a debt which had to be paid. This situation further facilitates in the psyche of the African American female the need to be independent and strong. If Matthew had only been responsible for his actions the outcome of this situation for his entire family could have been different. We as black males have to understand the root cause of our action towards our woman and our offspring and become removed from that learned behavior that derived from fear of separation. We must embrace our families with love and let nothing separate us from nurturing our young. As African Americans, we have not been able to comprehend that the head of household is the male. This is due to the historical destruction and disruption of the black male being out of the home first by force and later by choice. Examine the male-headed Caucasian traditional households in which male is the head and the woman fully trusts that he will make the right decisions for the family. We have to feel the same way about our black males, meaning see and acknowledge that they are strong and capable of being head of the household. Therefore, the African American females have an obligation as the mothers of our race to understand where insecurities about the African American males derived from and how to heal. You have an obligation to not put the government in situations that a responsible African American male and female can resolve. The evolution of our race depends upon us releasing this negative energy that slavery has placed on our race and freeing ourselves of these memories. We must understand why we are the way we are before we can fix the problem. Now we understand so let's unite as one people and fix the problems.

Lastly, slavery ushered in another great destroyer of our race which is inferiority. To feel inferior is to feel less than another or lower in rank compared to another. The Creator of all that is and the savior of mankind was always represented to black slaves as being white. Therefore, if God is white and the slave masters are white, then to be born black must be inferior. This had to be the perspective of slaves and this perspective is a part of the stored consciousness of the African American. When I speak of stored consciousness, I am talking about a part of our mind that operates separately from thought itself. It is the true governing principle of our lives. The outcome of this perspective being stored within us is a feeling of not belonging in certain establishments, a feeling that I must work harder or be perfect on my job, a feeling that predominantly white neighborhoods are better than black neighborhoods. The slave masters knew that to have black people worshipping a God that is white or the same color as they were would help them maintain their superiority for generations to come. But to place a color on the Creator is clearly a lack of spiritual and universal knowledge. We must understand that race divides came from the Caucasians and not the other humans on the planet.

When our ancestors saw the first white man they didn't see white they only saw a human with a lighter shade of hue. It was primarily the Caucasians that begin to label humans as races to distinguish their superiority among the races. This has had such a great effect on the African American community because we co-habitat with the Caucasians and were slaves for over 400 years to the Caucasians.

Even after being free for almost two generations, the inferiority trait is so deep in our race that it affects us in the professional world. I worked in corporate America for fifteen years and would oftentimes be the only African American person in a meeting and I would often wonder if I was worthy of being present. I would also wonder if they felt like I should or should not be present, all the long overlooking the sheer talent that I brought to the table. I have even spoken with African American doctors who oftentimes felt they might not be worthy to treat white patients or perform surgeries on white patients. Even college professors and teachers who had verbalized feeling inferior in the classroom based on race, or when asked a question by a white student wonder if they were worthy of answering their questions. All these aspects of inferiority derived from slavery and a loss of our identity as a race. Even when we spend thousands of dollars to attend the best universities, we enter the workforce still feeling inferior. This trait causes many of our African American college graduates to accept jobs that pay salaries slightly above the poverty lines. They end up owing thousands of dollars in student loans and with a job that pays 30,000 dollars a year. They often times marry and have kids on this meager salary and find it difficult to make ends meet. That is truly not what education is supposed to deliver, but we often times settle because we feel like we have no other choices. Our parents settled, their parents settle and that is the way it is. But just as you can recount the settling for less by your parents, your children will see the same in you. And when your children attend school and see Caucasian kids' parents in new cars, living nice homes, and nice clothes this reinforces the inferiority trait in our youth. Couple by having less and the constant reiteration of slavery to the African American youth by our educational system this trait becomes a part of our youth. The constant teaching of slavery in a classroom filled with both white and black youth constitutes the transference of power to the white youth and a feeling of inferiority to the blacks.

Our African American youth feels as though the white ancestors were superior to their own, then they too, as white children of those ancestors must also be superior to them. In elementary schools, the youth are equal in their perception of the world and their lives until the history of slavery is taught and then the children begin to see each other differently. There is a sense of superiority and inferiority that emerges along with the African American child noticing the financial inequality between his family and white families. Here you have the awakening of this inferiority trait from the stored consciousness of an African American youth. We must understand that this is a material world and to be born black with less constitutes two strikes or historically noted as 3/5ths a human, in either sense perpetuating a subpar human or so it is thought by our African American youth. But on the other hand, to be African American with more makes you more or closer to the Caucasians. I am not saying that we need to be a materialistic people, but I am saying that we must pick and choose our careers wisely and understand that in America money is what removes the inferiority trait and levels the battlefield in some ways. The only thing that has ever driven Caucasians to act is the love or lust of money and to have some is power. Therefore, when we are choosing our colleges and educational fields, we have to understand what is at stake. When we choose not to attend college and just to work we have to understand the seeds we are planting in that moment within our youth. After seeing and knowing that our ancestors were slaves, we should strive in every decision we make to strengthen our race and youth. The battle to remove inferiority can only be won by changing the perception of our youth and giving them hope and teaching them never to settle and to know their self-worth through all they have been taught.

# Chapter 2

# Segregation and its Effects

What is segregation and how did it really affect the African American race? Webster's dictionary defines segregation as the separation or isolation of a race, class, or ethnic group by enforced or voluntary residence in a restricted area, by barriers to social intercourse, by separate educational facilities, or by other discriminatory means. Several aspects of segregation in America were created by governmental actions. The government placed public housing in high-poverty areas, racially isolated neighborhoods, and allowed local governments to continue to treat blacks as slaves. They created a whites-only mortgage guarantee program that was designed to shift the white population to exclusive suburban neighborhoods. While refusing to sell well qualified black's houses in these predominantly white neighborhoods. All of these laws occurring during a time when blacks were freed from slavery with no education, no property, and no jobs. We as African Americans had nobody to invest in us not even the government; they wanted to keep us contained in a specific area and use our services as needed. We couldn't eat with them, use the same restrooms as they, drink from the same water fountain as them, but we could work on their farms from sun up to sun down and spend our money with them. A question that has gone unanswered throughout the years is why segregation was so important to the white population? What was the core reason for segregation?

The core reason for segregation was that the white population didn't want the mixing of blood between the two races. The Caucasians were well aware that if black was a dominant gene and white was a recessive gene when mixed the offspring would predominately be black. This insight alone diminishes the historical illusion of African Americans being inferior people. This one notion that we the African American race by simply having sexual intercourse with a Caucasian could begin to wipe a race from the planet was enough to want to keep us separate. The KKK and all white supremacy groups are well aware of this and that is why their hate is so deep. The African American race has never conducted any gruesome acts against white supremacy groups, but the hate groups hate African Americans as if they were committing murder against their children. But in truth African Americans have the power to do so and this is what fuels this fear. This is a deep seeded hatred. This is what kept the fire of segregation going. This is where the statement of keeping the Caucasian race pure derives from. We must understand we are not second-class human beings; we are dominant and able to change any race's offspring into the black. This is also why so many African Americans were beaten and hung for just looking at a white woman. Emmett Till was lynched in Mississippi just for supposedly whistling at a white woman. At this time Emmett was only 14 years old. An incident of this magnitude simply enhances our understanding of how deep-rooted this fear is and why segregation was widely supported by whites. I once knew a White man named John who was a hard-working farmer, but secretly John was a member of the local KKK chapter. John also hated black people and felt they should go back to Africa, he also taught this hatred to his children. John had a little girl and one son whom he consistently taught to despise blacks and Jews. John's daughter whose name was Lisa attended public schools where she was forced to interact with African Americans and ended up having African American friends. She knew if her father found out he would be disappointed and disown her. So during high school, she kept her friendships a secret and pretended to abide by her father's rules and pretended to share his views on blacks and Jews. After graduating from high school, Lisa found her a job and finally was able to move out of her parents' house. Her mother supported this move and helped Lisa to get settled into her new apartment. Several months later, Lisa fell in love with an African American male who worked at her job and she became pregnant for the young man. Lisa informed her mother, but not her father about her situation because she knew her father would not approve of a mixed baby and would demand an abortion. Lisa and her mother were able to maintain the secret until her pregnancy began to show. Her father was ecstatic when he found out he would be a grandfather until the day before Lisa was scheduled to give birth. Lisa and her mother informed John that his grandchild had a black father. This information was too difficult for John to accept; he was furious and disowned both his wife and his daughter. This situation went against everything he believed and was his fear born into his reality. His only daughter was having a baby that would be considered by his peers to be black or a nigger.

John divorced his wife of twenty-five years, did not speak to his only daughter any more, or never saw his newly born grandchild. John was deeply hurt by what had happened and he felt portrayed by those he had loved. He continued to spend time with his son to try to minimize his inner pain, but nothing he did could ease the pain. Two years had passed and he still had not spoken with his wife or daughter. John was ashamed to even attend his KKK meetings he felt his life was ruined. John finally died of a heart attack after living the last two years of his life as a hermit. John and other people like John are not aware that what they fear or hate must someday become an experience. Therefore those who supported segregation at some point will be segregated against. But I have to ask was segregation that terrible for the African American race or could we have created a world of our own? Was becoming desegregated so important to us because we truly wanted to be like our slave masters or was it truly about equal rights? Could we have created our own thriving society if so would the Caucasians allow a successful black community to exist?

One of the greatest terror attacks in the history of the United States was conducted by the klutz Klux Klan in Tulsa Oklahoma. This attack was conducted on a thriving black community called Black Wall Street. This community had over 600 successful black businesses 21 churches, 21 restaurants, 30 grocery stores, a hospital, libraries, schools, law offices, private planes, jewelry stores, 2 movie theaters, and a bus system. With a population of 15,000 African Americans in this community, the dollar would circulate 36 to 100 times before leaving the community, sometimes taking a year to leave the community. It currently only takes the dollar 6 hours to leave the black community 17 days to leave white communities and 20 days to leave the Jewish community. This was one of the first thriving black communities and there were many more like this one, but our race is only shown the poverty-stricken black communities longing to segregate with the whites hoping for a better life. We have not been shown that in the past, there had been some African American communities that had been capable of building wealth without being desegregated. On June 1, 1921, this community was bombed from the air and burned by angry whites. The anger derived from the notion of a former slave being wealthier than a white person and that we could build successful infrastructures. In approximately 12 hours, 36 business districts lay burned to the ground and 3000 African Americans were dead. This massacre is unknown by the majority of our race and erased from the history books. The fact that former slaves could unite and build great communities together in which we did not depend on whites, instead we depended on each other was a scary notion to some. So, if we could unite and build successful infrastructures why desegregate?

We needed to desegregate for protection under the law that all citizens needed to thrive in this country. You see we could have never built a sustainable successful black community because whites would either take it from us or just destroy it. And during this time there was no penalty for hanging, burning or taking property from a black person. Our children were unjustly killed, our land was taken, we were incarcerated just for the states to retain free labor; therefore we needed the protection of the government. But once we had those laws to truly protect us did we really need to be desegregated or could this have naturally occurred without the sacrifices our ancestors made?

During slavery, a slave was only considered to be 3/5ths of a human being. We were not even considered by the constitution to be fully a human being. So where did our ancestors get their self-worth from? It was definitely not the government; therefore it was the former slave owners. The biggest slaves, the lighter skinned slaves, the hardest working slave all were worth more to the slave owners. This distorted view by our ancestors of self-worth is why desegregation was so important. We wanted to be viewed as a human by our former slave owners and we were still in the mental construct of defining our self-worth by how our slave masters viewed us. Over the four hundred years of slavery, we had lost our self-truths and the fact that self-worth comes from within and not without. That is why there were a few thriving black societies during this time because they no longer sought self-worth from their former slave master. They understood that self-worth was internal and went on to create a better life for themselves and their families. Even those that marched with Dr. Martin Luther King Jr. understood the importance of self-worth; they were willing to lose their lives to defend their self-worth. They understood what the former slave masters thought their lives were worth, but were willing to die to prove them differently. On the other hand, the majority of our race was still in the slave mindset and was comfortable defining their self-worth through the lens of their former slave master. A prime example of this is when a Caucasian calls a black person a Nigger. The black person gets angry, aggressive, and defensive. But why does this occur in the individual? The individual has never truly experienced the horrors of slavery and more than likely has never had to give up his belongings for being black. The reason these emotions arise is because something in this particular individual is still allowing the former slave master to define his self-worth, therefore anger occurs. But, an individual that is truly in tune with himself only sees the ignorance in such a statement. And no anger arises within that individual because he understands that the opinion of another has no bearing on his reality and self-worth. This was and still is the cancer that plagues the collective consciousness of the African American experience. This exists only because there are some that still think their self-worth is defined by what their Caucasian boss thinks of them just as our ancestors strived to be liked by their former slave masters. In this longing for acceptance, we lose power and surrender power over our lives to them. You begin to take their thoughts of you to be true, you are destroyed or built up by their words, and you think the well- being of your life derives from what they allow you to have. This simply means your reality has been distorted and you are not in control of your life just as our ancestors had seemingly lost control of theirs. Every action against the African American people has been a seed that we simply allow to grow within our collective consciousness. When we don't look inside ourselves we water and tend to these seeds. You see we give these seeds life and allow them to grow from generation to generation. We have to look inward to find these seeds and dig them up and remove them. This is the only way we can be free and the only way our true self-worth can be defined.

Over the years we have allowed our collective consciousness to become sponge-like, soaking up all kinds of trash and allowing it to manifest in our reality. We have given words like Nigger power over us and the ability to disrupt our reality. A prime example of the true nature of words is DR. Masaru Emoto's rice experiment. In this experiment, Dr. Emoto placed rice in three different containers along with crystallized water. He then labeled each container one with love and good words, one with hate and bad words, and the last container he totally ignored. Over time, the rice labeled with love and good words continued to be white and had not decomposed; the rice that he spoke bad words to have turned black and began to decompose, and the rice he ignored had totally decomposed and was rotten. These experiments have shown how water reacts to words and the human body is about 75% water therefore if allowed words will have a bearing on our consciousness also. And this is what has happened to the African American race, over time words such as nigger, darkie, porch monkey, worthlessness, lazy have all attacked our consciousness. This attack has caused our reality to be distorted because we have let these words become seeds and these seeds have become strongholds in our souls. I once heard from a friend about an African American male named Earl who was called a Nigger by a white male while attending a sporting event. They both were cheering for different teams and this is where the disputed originated from. During a heated argument between the two adults the white male called Earl a nigger. It was said that when Earl was called a Nigger, he verbalized and described the feeling as a knife cutting through his soul and his mind went blank. He immediately tried to assault the man for insulting him with the word Nigger, but luckily his friends who had attended the game with Earl had stopped him. Earl had given the power to control his consciousness to a word. No word has the power to make us react in a certain manner unless we give it the power to. Therefore, humanity has the power to reject words, and not allow them to cause emotions to erupt within us due to another referring to us in a certain manner. In Proverbs chapter 4 verse 23 in the Holy Bible states **(More than anything you guard, protect your mind, for life flows from it)**. What type of life can flow from a disease mental construct? What type of life flows from a mind that is controlled by what another race thinks or feels you are worth? What type of life flows from a mind that desires to assimilate another and not look inside and become all we were sent here to be?

In short, both segregation and slavery were defining moments in the diminishing of the mental construct of the African American people. And this is because we became defined by these actions, in other words, our self-worth was defined by these two actions. And during these actions we allowed strongholds to form in our collective consciousness that we are still fighting to remove. All of this occurred because we couldn't comprehend what the universe or the Creator was transforming our race into. When construction workers begin to build a building the first things that they have to build is the foundation. The foundation of the building is the deciding factor on how much weight and just how strong that build will be upon completion. And this is the same construct the Creator used in the construct of the African American race. Our foundation is the strongest foundation in the world, we have endured slavery and segregation and we still push on. Our foundation is a testimony of how beautiful and strong our buildings will be when we allow our Creator to complete the construction of our race. But as we speak more seeds are being planted, therefore the first and most important step is to guard what we allow into our minds because it will slowly transform into our reality.

# Chapter 3
# The Media Effects

Since the conception of mass communication, the media have been waging war on the collective consciousness of the African American population. The media use radio, newspapers, television, social media and music to manipulate our perception of reality. The media are so powerful it has had the ability to implant beliefs into a society without the society even being aware of it. A prime example of this power is clothing styles or shoes. The media has the ability glorify a certain type of clothes or shoes just by allowing a famous person to wear these styles and by repetitively showing these ads. Eventually, these clothes become the new fad. This is no different from what the media does to our mental construct. The media is a very powerful construct and it has been used over and over again to tear the African American race down and built us back up into what it desires us to be by repetitively sending a message. The media feeds our subconscious mind without us being aware that is why it is so powerful.

We will start our journey into this war with a look at when the media began its attack on the African American race. It begins when a child becomes intelligent enough to hold their attention on a television show. A child then begins to watch cartoons that depict the world of white kids or fictional characters filled with an abundance of toys, family vacations, multiple cars, upstairs homes, and a household with both parents. They portray the characters living in beautiful neighborhoods, staying in nice homes, and having the freedom to experience whatever their hearts desire. But on the other hand, in the lives of most our African American children these constructs do not exist. There are only a few African American kids that grow up in this manner and even those are familiar with the ghettos in their cities. But so many of the African American kids stay in housing projects, or low income housing where crime has become an everyday part of life. The fathers are not present in the home and are not an active part of their little lives. There are not many vacations because their families are not able to afford them, and there is not an abundance of material things in their lives. The neighborhood's streets are littered with trash, there are alcoholics better known as inner-city drunks roaming the streets, and drug-addicted individuals searching for their next high. But take in consideration the cartoons are repetitively depicting to the child how life is supposed to be which is entirely different from the reality they know. The child begins to wonder why his or her life is so different and the only difference a child can see or understand is color. There are not many whites in these types of neighborhoods so through what little deductive reasoning they have they now see their color as probable deficiency. They also can now correlate wealth with happiness and a more pleasing life. Both these concepts slowly become strongholds to the realities of our children. When our youth at such a young tender age think because they are African American they are at a disadvantage not advantage and wealth is the key to happiness the future of the African American race becomes tainted. This is because by the age of seven our subconscious minds have already established its core beliefs and these beliefs become the governing factors of our lives. The media understand this one aspect of how depicting a life different from the one our youth is custom to affects how they think and that how we as a people thinks affects our reality, that is why our youth is attack before the age of five or attending school. But when we examine this paradigm closer we realize that the media lacks the understanding of how such ideology helps our race strive for greatness. You see if our children were not aware that there is a better life than poverty then what would they strive for. If being wealthy had not ever been introduced to the consciousness of the African American youth then they would not even understand the concept. This is no different than hot would not exist without the understanding of cold. So, in essence if we are raising our youth in poverty we must allow them to see that there is better and allow them to strive for it, but most of all we must closely examine how our youth is absorbing this information into their subconscious minds. We as the parents must determine at an early age if our youth are using these cartoons to strive for better or have these cartoon created a negative disposition in their lives. If we see a negative disposition being created in our youth we must at once attack that negative disposition and ensure our youth understands that they must change these negative thought patterns into positive thought patterns that cause them to strive for greatness. We the parents are blind and do not see what the media is busy doing to our youth. We don't understand that once these strongholds are established, they are difficult to destroy therefore we must help our youth to see their probable deficiencies as opportunities to grow and not a death sentence. One thing we do know is that we are not actively teaching our African American youth at such a young age that it is a disadvantage to be African American.

Next, the children become of age and then attend schools and read different literature which does not help them to understand themselves and the world around them. Suddenly they began to learn about slavery and segregation. This reignites those earlier thoughts that being an African American is a type of racial deficiency. They read and see what their ancestors and in some cases their great-great grandparents had to endure. In a classroom setting where these subjects are taught, where there are both Caucasian and African American children, there is a shift that begins to take place in that moment. This shift reduces the amount of power the African American children feel they have inside and around them. The white kids are introduced to historical facts that support their supremacy over the African American and this supremacy has been in place for over 400 years. They see that only because of their ancestors' leanantacy is an entire race of people now free. They also see that through this same leanantacy did an entire race receive the rights to vote or even be seated in a restaurant for dinner. They see their power and understand that the world is theirs for the taking. They now have the perception that because of history there is no African American no matter who he is or what he has accomplished is equal to them because they are white. On the other hand, the message received from the information about slavery by the African American children is very different. They now see that their ancestors were captured and enslaved. They were forced to work for free and treated worse than the plantation dog. They were beaten, hung, and often times children separated from their families. They also see that everything that was precious to human life was taken away from their ancestors. And because of the grace of the Northern States and the Civil War, their ancestors were freed. In other words, they see their ancestors were granted freedom by other white people. Then the African American youth learns about segregation where African Americans were considered animals and not allowed to drink from the same water fountain or use the same restroom facilities as whites. They could not vote, were quarantined in ghettos, and were still being hunted down and hung as though slavery still existed. They learn that African Americans had to ride on the back of the bus as second-class citizens, could not attend a white school, and could not play sports in white leagues. They learn about the marches in Alabama, where blacks were beaten, attacked by dogs, and sprayed with high-pressure water hoses only because they wanted equal rights. And then, all of a sudden by the grace of the white man segregation ends. What do you think has happened to the pride and strength of these African American youths? Their pride and sense of power have diminished and they now subconsciously think that being an African American is a disadvantage and that all through history whites were superior to blacks. In some of these kids, anger or resentment may occur, but the underlying message will be received fully intact. The message is that African American were and still are powerless and this message is repetitive and poisoning our youth. The truth is, almost all races were slaves at some point in their evolution. So why is it so important to reiterate this to the African American and Caucasian youth simultaneously? And the answer is inferiority and the implanting of this seed in every African American child's brain. The powers that be understand that if we think a certain way, then that becomes our reality. We must teach our children that even though their ancestors endured such cruelty that is not their life, but only a part of their foundation. They are an entirely different soul sent here to experience an entirely different reality. They must understand that their ancestors enduring slavery was a part of a universal plan that gave birth to a new race whose future is still unfolding. As the African American race continues to evolve, we will discover that the pain and suffering our ancestors endured was not in vain, but in fact in evolution pain is an important precursor for growth. The book of Exodus in the Biblical scriptures depicts how the Jews evolved from slavery and pain into a race of people who were given their own land to dwell. And now, a large part of wealth in the United States of America is owned by Jews. This is called race evolution. This story is no different than what we have happening at this moment in the African American evolution. Therefore, we must teach them that there are truly no boundaries and that their freedom does not come from the decisions of a race but from a life force that all beings share. They must understand that history is just what it says, it is his-story. But in order for the African American race to even see or understand these mental traps, we have to elevate our collective consciousness to a level where we are above mortal thought patterns. We must evolve to a level where we are able to conceptualize a bright future for our race and it begins with the battle for our youth. Are you prepared to fight? Are you mentally equipped enough to make a difference or will we continue to lose at the starting block of the race of life?

The next attack occurs when our youth becomes a teenager and begins to understand his or her environment and listen to music that is from his culture. In their environments, there are some positive attributes that the music his culture produces can derive from, but the record executives deem these attributes as unmarketable. In other words, the positive music is not even entertained by most record companies. If you can recall our music was called soul because it derived from one's soul and you could feel it deep within your being. Even when rap music first came on the scene, it was positive and about having fun. We made love music that talked about beautiful relationships between a man and a woman. We didn't call our women bitches and hoes and treat them in demeaning ways. But now leap forward into 2017 and all of this is gone. The music still exists within us, but it never makes it to the mainstream media because this isn't the part of the African American culture that the media want to glorify. The powers that be understand that glorifying the good attributes that are present in the black culture would slowly cause a shift in the collective consciousness of our youth. They would begin to love and respect woman, themselves, and others. Therefore, strengthen instead of weakening a race of people. So instead the record companies produce music that glorifies drug abuse, guns, gangs, sexuality and treating our African American queens as trash. They also glorify expensive cars, jewelry, clothes, and homes all of which are designed to maintain the excessive spending of the African American race.  All of these behaviors can only destroy a race of people, especially when it is introduced to our youth at a young age.

Hip Hop started out as a positive means of expression for the African American community. It also brought some of our poor inner-city youths into wealth and they in return help others get out of the ghetto. It was because of this ability it caught on like wildfire in the communities. Hip-hop was a pillar of the African American community; it was fun to watch battle raps and uplifting to listen to. It had the ability to bring blacks together; we danced, laughed and enjoyed each other's company. But when it was noted how this could change our community for the better, it was attacked. The music that was once a pillar of the community was turned into a destroyer of our community. We now see that our hip-hop culture glorifies drug use, becoming gang members, drug dealing, guns, material wealth, and demeaning women. And most of our hip-hop artists fail to understand what this type of music is doing to our youth. This music may not affect all African American youth, but it destroys a considerable amount on a daily basis. This is because it is glorifying everything that leads to African American males becoming incarcerated or becoming addicted to drugs and African American females thinking they must expose their bodies to be considered beautiful. Our music is used to brainwash our youth into thinking drug abuse, drug dealing, gangs, guns, and material wealth are a way of life. When our youth repetitively listens to music that promotes such content they begin to feel compelled to live this lifestyle. I once knew a young man named Robert who was a high school basketball star. Robert had several colleges interested in him after his performance in his junior year in high school in which he had averaged twenty-five points per game. Robert and his friends loved to listen to hip-hop music that talked about smoking marijuana and popping pills. The music had somehow attacked their subconscious minds and now they felt this was cool. They slowly begin to smoke weed and weeks later begin to experiment with a pill called Molly. Robert's basketball performances begin to suffer, and people wondered what had happened. About halfway through his senior high school season, Robert was placed on the bench for his poor performance. He also lost all his opportunities for obtaining a scholarship to play basketball in college. Upon graduation, he became addicted to Molly and marijuana and had to be placed in rehab. Robert also began to suffer from psychosis due to his drug abuse and was admitted to a mental health facility. Robert is currently working hard to get his life back on track. Before he could realize what was happening in his life three years of drug abuse had robbed him of everything he had worked hard as a teenager to gain. This is just one case of a youth who took the lyrics of the music he chose to listen to literally and decided to try the drugs, but we must understand there are many Roberts out there in the world. When our youth focus, take in and live by the laws of this destructive music literally they begin to sell drugs, do drugs, join gangs, carry guns, rob each other, and even commit murders. Most of our artists cannot see the correlation between our music, the judicial system, and correctional facilities. The media is using our music as a catalyst to make more money from the African American people. Here is how it works, when the African American youth begin to commit crimes in a localized area, this area in the city becomes labeled a high crime area, and it is then thoroughly patrolled by law enforcement agents. Young African American men and women are charged with crimes and placed in jail awaiting court dates. Parents and loved ones are forced to post their bails so that they can receive their freedom back until their court dates. And if the families cannot afford to post bails, then the youth may sit in jail for weeks even months awaiting trial. This is money being fed into the judicial system or the bail bonds. This is money that is now not present in the African American communities. Next, very few of the youth will have the funds to obtain a lawyer, so, one will be appointed to represent them. They will have a jury appointed to them who is not familiar with their culture or the environment that they grew up in. Their jury will consist of mostly Caucasians whom life is totally different from theirs and whose perception is different. And this is because of the jury selection process and the number of African Americans with felonies, therefore, cannot participate in trials. The youth is therefore found guilty and sentenced to prison and fined by the state. In this instance, we have more money being fed into the judicial system, a loss of freedom, free labor for the state, and money for privatized prisons. Can you see how we are losing the attack on our youth and our culture? We must understand that the media are making a selected few of us rich, but at the same time are using our music to destroy our race. They are making money from the labor and our musical talents, funding the judicial system; the state receives free labor, and funding privatized prisons all with the African American race. Aren't we aware that people are buying stocks in privatized prisons? Therefore, there must be expectations that they will one day be filled. And most important of all, we must understand that in the United States, we are only 13% of the population, but we make up 35% of jail inmates and 38% of prison inmates. For every single rapper that makes it and glorifies destructive attributes in his music, he takes down hundreds or even thousands of us in some form or fashion. This is no different from the evolution of slavery; they used us against one another in exchange for material wealth. And we are allowing history to repeat itself right now.

The greatest way that the entertainment industry is using our music to make money is hip-hop videos. The powers that be understand that African Americans have a psychological disposition, which is the need to be noticed or viewed as a person with money. For that reason alone, they use our hip hop videos to introduce new trends to the black community and make profits. They make profits because they understand that the African Americans buy by brand and quality and this is what they portray our artists as having in hip-hop videos. They wear brand name watches, wear diamond necklaces, brand name clothes and shoes, and drive foreign cars. Although most of the rappers do not own the items in the videos it still sets a standard for the African American and it is one that most try hard to achieve. The weapon is so powerful that when a new fad becomes popular hip-hop investors begin to buy stock in the items deemed as hip-hop fads because they know the

African American will sacrifice everything to be perceived by others as an individual with material wealth. Therefore, they know they will receive a return on their money. But we must understand it is not the artists who are guilty because they are also being destroyed by the exact industry they serve. This because once they shoot their first video with all the jewelry, expensive clothes, and foreign cars, then they too attempt to live that life. In a sense, the artists are being brainwashed also by being introduced to such a lifestyle that he or she will now chase. The powers that be know that he will not put money back into his community, at least not enough to make a change. They are aware that the African American artist may occasionally give a little to his or her community, but the majority will go back to large white-owned businesses. This is because the desire to be noticed has been a generational disease in the African American community that has not been cured. And it continues to ruin lives and take our collective ability to gain and maintain wealth. All of these actions go back to the African American's mental disposition acquired from slavery and segregations. During these periods blacks were not able to experience the more expensive things in life and this has created a disposition of if I can get it I will get it. And if I get it, I will be seen from a different vantage point which is of importance and wealth. We do not understand the importance of investing and creating jobs in our own communities. If an African American artist had acquired 500,000 dollars it is highly unlikely he will purchase a business in a black community, but more likely he will purchase some jewelry and a Bentley. In this instance, he is not growing spiritually, and neither is his community growing financially.

The hip-hop videos not only bring in new fads, but these fads affect our youth in a negative way. The clothes and styles that the hip-hop videos glorify then cause our youth to begin to wear, create obstacles for our youth in obtaining jobs in American companies. This problem occurs because most of these styles are associated with people who are thugs and gangsters. Therefore, when our youths wear these clothes or fads from the hip-hop videos they are stereotyped by society and are not considered for upper-level jobs. But, if no one had created an image of what being a thug looks like then there would be no thug just some youth that dressed differently. But hip-hop videos have given Caucasians and African Americans the imagery of what a thug looks like and this has plagued our communities. When our youth thinks having multiple gold teeth in their mouth is a positive thing and tries to get a job they are usually not taken seriously by the hiring entity of that company. When they wear their pants hanging off their behinds showing their underwear they are not taken seriously for any job and their input in any situation is not deemed as wise. When their hair is in a certain style this also eliminates them from being considered for employment. And usually, if they are able to find jobs they only pay minimum wage. Therefore, it still becomes difficult to change their financial status. A considerable number of our youth is embracing these dressing ideas from the hip-hop culture and do not understand that these dress codes can impede progressions in the real society. And as we buy these new types of clothing we are putting our hard earned dollars back into the hands from which it came and haven't improved our communities at all. And these fashion statements are looked down upon by society, therefore hindering our youth from being able to obtain good positions within a company which could possibly yield wealth and the ability to own property. Our female youth view these videos and see women dressed in clothes that expose their bodies and they feel they have to dress this way to be relevant or beautiful. They feel that if they expose their bodies, maybe they will find a young man with money who will change their financial situation. Now then we have young women not trying to look inside themselves to improve, but exposing her body which is sacred in hopes that her improvement will come from a man. There are always underlying factors that have the ability to lead us as a race astray if we are not focused and have created our own self-concept. Therefore we must begin to ask questions to remove ourselves from the fog. Why do rappers have to dress a certain way and wear all kinds of jewelry? Why do the women in their videos expose their bodies? Why do they have to act in an aggressive manner or be seen as gangsters? What if the rappers wore suits and the women dressed dignified, what message would that send? You see these are the questions that have the power to awaken a sleeping culture. We are battling principles that we must begin to understand because this is where our future lies. What are we prepared to do to stop these attacks? Can't we see that our music has taken us from a people that dressed dignified, and a race with moral standards, to a people with sagging pants with our underwear showing? This is how powerful music can be. It has taken us from a dignified people to a people who barely understand what it means to have dignity in ones' self and pride in our neighborhoods. Now that we have connected the dots and we can see our demise we must demand better music and stop supporting music that destroys our race. The media is all about money and if we don't purchase or support the music that destroys our culture, it will dissolve and allow our collective consciousness to shift.

A famous scholar once said that the eyes are the window to the soul, and this is where the media uses television. We must understand that if we only read books about slavery, we could only visualize what slavery really was like. That visualization would be filtered by our brains, and would only depict slavery in a way that is tolerable by each individual soul. But television skips that filter by using the eyes to make an impression directly on the subconscious mind. Therefore, when we make movies about slavery and segregations the individual watching these movies are generally experiencing slavery because the eyes are able to see it, therefore forcing our brains to process it. Now in this form, it truly becomes a part of our realities and begins to facilitate a loss of power in a specific person or race of people. When we see a slave being hung or beaten in a movie this forces our brain to come to terms with the pain and suffering associated with that experience. This is much different than simply reading about such an incident. This is because in reading you cannot see the facial expressions of the victim being beaten or hung. You cannot see the tears in his eyes and the hopelessness in his face. You cannot see his torn clothes, bruised back, and callused hands by reading a book. But when looking at a movie the brain processes every facial expression, every tear, and every bruise. The pain becomes real and grows into hatred caused by knowing that because of the color of their skin they were subject to this abuse. But in the realization of this pain, there is a loss of power that occurs in the African American. And there is also the realization of the inferiority associated with being black. Pain, hatred, and inferiority are all low-frequency emotions. These emotions drag human consciousness level down and keep them imprisoned. To break out of this prison often times takes years of inner engineering to remove these blocks and some even a lifetime. These emotions have the ability to guide the human perception of the physical world. For example, when the individual is around whites, he feels inferior or even not worthy no matter what sacrifices he made to get there. He cannot see his own self-worth or what he brings to the table, in other words, his perception is diseased therefore his reality is diseased. The media understand how watching such shows and movies affect the African American community, therefore, they keep producing them and bring up new aspects of slavery and segregation. We as parents of African American youth have a responsibility to only allow our kids to read about the atrocities of slavery and never allow them to be infiltrated by movies or shows. This is because pain and suffering are energies that are able to be transferred simply by the eyes viewing and the subconscious mind receiving. Once this energy is present in the subconscious minds of our youth it begins to plant seeds of inferiority, inequality, and hatred. In order to truly understand this concept, we must understand the subconscious mind and how it operates. The subconscious mind remembers all events in our lives from our inception to our death. It records all words spoken and all events witnessed by the eyes. It does not determine whether the words spoken have true intentions behind them or if an event is truly happening or being viewed on television. It just simply records everything and considers it to be true; therefore it is important to be aware of what we say, and what events we are experiencing. This is because the universal mind, we all possess is recording our every action, every thought, and every word spoken. So when we watch movies about slavery and we begin to think in a certain manner about the atrocities of slavery, then we speak in a certain manner about slavery, and we allow these movies to cause our emotions to boil our subconscious mind is recording these actions and the event of slavery becomes real to us. Once we allow our past event to plant seeds within us or our youth these seeds grow and we become often times consumed with attempting to correct the past which no longer exists. I once had a really close friend named Oscar, who enjoyed watching movies about slavery such as Roots, and 12 years a slave. He also enjoyed reading books about slavery and had a library in his house filled with books containing this type of material. Over a period of time after constantly feeding his subconscious mind this type of material, there was a shift in consciousness that happened in Oscar. He began to hate white people and also begin to think that he was still living in some form of slavery. Oscar became a civil rights activist, but his goal was not to protect the current rights of African American but to get reparation for slavery. In other words, Oscar was still focused on the past and not looking forward to a bright future. The seeds had grown within him and changed his perception of the world around him. He had become a man who was fighting seeds that he himself had planted. Therefore, we as African Americans must be careful of what we give our attention to because when we are consumed by events we truly do not understand we plant seeds that distort our perception and we become imprisoned in our own reality.

The creation of the internet allowed the entire world to communicate and the creation of social media brought friends and like-minded people together in groups. Both of these aspects are positive, but we will only discuss the aspects that affect us negatively. The first negative aspect is it consumes our awareness of the world around us. Most people become so consumed in searching the internet or on social media hours of time past by without them even realizing the amount of time lost. If a person is on social media or the internet, two hours a day then that ends up to be fourteen hours per week and 56 hours per month. To put it in a greater perspective, this person would lose 728 hours per year or 30 days per year. In other words, this person is aware of his or her surroundings only 11 months out of the entire year. They have lost an entire month that could have been used to learn a new skill, read a book, or spend time with loved ones. But instead, they have used their time on social media and the internet viewing things that already have strongholds in his or her reality. We must understand that social media and the internet give these mental strongholds access to an unlimited amount of information and videos that increase the stronghold's power over our perception. In other words, if a person likes porn he or she has access to an unlimited amount on the internet. But when the individual spends 30 days out of the year watching porn the stronghold grows and will eventually boil over into a criminal act. If a person likes drugs, fights, or a materialistic lifestyle, that individual will find like-minded people and an unlimited amount of videos on the internet or social media. Also, if there is a lifestyle a person wants to live he or she can act as if they are living that lifestyle by posting fake pictures, posting messages that portray themselves a certain way, and posting live videos. But even in portraying a fake lifestyle the stronghold of wanting life to be different grows its power also. It is important to understand what it truly means to have immediate access to view what we desire. Furthermore is critical to the individual to understand that desire and examine it closely. Normally this unquenchable desire is a stronghold within us that must be conquered and using the internet to view or search this topic only gives it more power over our realities. To thoroughly understand this concept we must go back to a time before the inception of the internet. If a person addicted to porn wanted to experience porn they would have had to go into a store and purchase a pornographic magazine or a VCR tape to view porn. The human interaction alone would deter a normal reasoning person from entering a store daily and purchasing magazines and VCR tapes. This is simply because they would feel that the people working in the store would become aware of their porn addiction and begin to judge them. The human ego or the strongholds that govern our realities like to go undetected therefore they protect themselves from being discovered by others. Also, another limiting aspect would be the daily spending of money to obtain these items. But if we fast forward into today's time we see that the internet has destroyed these buffers and now there is truly no deterrent for an individual addicted to porn. He or she may view porn for free any time and any place, this only gives unlimited power over that person's reality to the stronghold that already has his consciousness imprisoned. We must understand that this unlimited access used by a diseased mind only pushes us further away from experiencing true reality. It only increases the thickness of the walls surrounding the higher self that dwells within each and every one of us. It decreases the light that shines within us and increases the power of the strongholds over our personalities. Therefore whatever we search on the internet, post on social media, or view, we must be mindful of it and how it could affect our consciousness. We must ask ourselves why are we searching and viewing a certain topic. If this question is asked with an open mind and a desire to be free one may discover a stronghold that is holding them captive and finally obtain freedom. We must also ask ourselves, will this topic build us up or eventually tear us down? These questions will deter us from posting fights, videos of a sexual content, and viewing topics that will not help us to grow.

We the African American race must grasp these concepts of how important it is to be capable of seeing behind the veil mass media has placed in front of our faces. And we must also understand that as technology grows there will be new and more advanced ways to attack our reality. You see, our reality is the only thing in this world that is truly ours, but it is ours only if we are present in every moment and grounded in who we are. The media can only attack the mental aspect of who we are and this is why protecting our youth is so important. Our youth is still in the process of finding who they truly are when they become under attack. Therefore, we must be steadfast in what our youth view on television, types of music they listen to, and the educational systems they are attending. All is not lost, but if we don't wake up as a people, another 400 years will pass and we will still own only 1.5% of the nation's wealth which is the same as it was during slavery.

# Chapter 4

# The Effects of Police Brutality

Historically, in the evolution of the African American race, the police have been portrayed as an obstacle that stands between us and our freedom of expression and equal rights. Studies also indicate that African Americans are 3.5% more likely to be killed by police than whites. And that, 1 in 60,000 blacks is killed by police and 1 in 200,000 whites are killed by police. But the odds of a police officer being killed by an African American are 1 in a million, which is literally a non-existing issue. So why have so many African Americans been killed in the last couple of years by the police and no officers have been prosecuted for these killings? These killings receive media coverage and the entire world observes the racial profiling that happens in our communities and yet no one is held responsible for the loss of life. The families of the deceased will be haunted by this tragedy for the rest of their lives, but what's even more concerning, is the children of the deceased. How will the children of the deceased now perceive the police? Will the children respect the authority of the police or will they despise policing all together? Will law enforcement be seen as the protector of the public or someone who takes the freedom of African Americans or even kill them senselessly? How will this subconsciously affect the African American people who are involved in the marches or those who watched the news daily to see the outcome? The entire world is watching how the African American experience is unfolding in the United States but no one is helping. Every day on social media sites there are videos of what appears to be police brutality against black people without any repercussions for these actions. Even though these videos have thousands of views both foreign and domestic no disciplinary actions are taken to rectify these issues. How can this be happening in the land in which all citizens are free? And what are those who are watching these videos subconsciously receiving?

In the universe, there are two emotions that all other emotions derive from, and they are love and fear. Every action we take in our lives will derive from one or the other. Some examples we experience of love are joy, happiness, trust, gratitude, belonging, and peace. Some examples of fear are hate, falsehood, fearfulness, anxiety, sadness, mistrust, and lack. The underlying vibrational frequency associated with police injustices is fear. And when a group of people or race operates in fear the perception of reality becomes distorted. But not only does fear have to be present in the police involved, it also has to be present in the victim as well in order for a life to be taken in an encounter between law enforcement and a civilian. So how did this fear become the driving force in police brutality?

Fear in white police derived from slavery, therefore there was a belief that their ancestors had that still exists today. That belief was that blacks were truly stronger, faster, and more animal-like than whites, therefore, had to be controlled by any means necessary. Those blacks were animals or were as strong as animals and could not be confronted alone. That their endurance of pain and physical labor was superior to that of the white race, therefore physical confrontations would not be favorable for whites. The plantation owners feared that the slaves who were stronger and oftentimes outnumbered them would one day take over the plantations killing the masters. There was an element of control that the slave owners treasured and feared losing. Therefore the slave masters would pay poor whites to police the slaves while they were working in the fields and also to capture runaway slaves. But the problem was the poor whites also feared confrontations without guns or means to maintain control. And often times this fear caused them to utilize deadly force on slaves or even pushed them to hang the slaves. The wives of the slave masters often times feared the slaves as well and felt the need to be protected or feel safe. The violence of slavery is a direct correlation of the vibration of fear. The whites during this time felt that they were weaker and feared that they one day would lose control. Fear is a low vibrating frequency that manifests its self in the perpetrator as acts of violence or aggression. This fear has survived for over 400 years and has become a growing issue in America. This country has had an African American President that served two terms, and there are multiple blacks in politics. Also, there are multiple African Americans that dominate the entertainment industry, both music, and movies, also sports. There are African American CEOs of large companies and hold other prestigious positions in our growing economy. Therefore, some Caucasians feel that what their forefathers had feared in slavery is slowly becoming a reality. This fear is that the control of the White male in American is slowly disintegrating; therefore it must be protected at all cost. This is the one fear that is currently keeping White Supremacy organizations thriving today. And this is also where our police brutality issues solely derive from. Our police are subconsciously acting out of fear, therefore, simple police stops or investigations conducted on blacks have the ability to escalate all the way to deadly force. They feel these situations must be controlled at all cost even if lesser measures could have been used to gain control of the suspect. These police officers still possess the mental disposition of the poor whites during slavery that was hired to protect the plantations. The plantation has now changed from an estate that is owned by a single individual to an entire city. And these police who are guilty of conducting themselves in a manner that constitutes police brutality solely against African Americans are acting from a disposition that they must maintain white control. If the police officer is then indicted for the extreme use of force, the jury will be all white due to the jury selection process in most states. Therefore, it becomes increasingly easy for the defendant's attorney to sell the all-white jury on the old slavery theme that a crazed

Negro was on the loose and had to be subdued at all cost. The truth of the matter is that the fear of a crazed Negro that derived from slavery is still alive in the white community today. It has been reported by numerous amounts of blacks that when they walk by whites sitting in cars they can hear them locking their doors because of fear. Also, Officer Wilson stated that during his encounter with the deceased Michael Brown that during the incident, Brown had an intense aggressive face that looked like a demon. This statement clearly shows the existence of some deep-rooted fear, and because of this fear deadly force was used. We are operating with a fear-based judicial system that destroys the lives of citizens and innocent people solely to maintain the illusion of control. Now we have another black life lost, a community now mourning the loss of their loved ones, and the entire world watching the African American experience.

These altercations between African American and the police are highly publicized not just to inform everyone of the incident, but to also send a message subliminally to the black race. This message is, no matter how great you become you are still a second class citizen in America. And that your children can be videoed being killed by police and nothing will happen. The cop will go free and you will be left morning just as your ancestors did during slavery when they were separated from their children. This fear ripples through the African American communities, forcing them to revisit the destructive pain of slavery and segregation. And in some African Americans, it erupts in anger and aggression. This oftentimes causes riots and some forms of retaliation which are met by a police show of force or even action if warranted.   Fearfulness and anger are both vibrations of fear, therefore these emotions will manifest negatively in the physical reality. It will manifest in the form of a loss of life, a loss of freedom, or a police losing his or her job. These police and African American interactions contain all the aspects of fear because if the vibration of love was present these interactions would be respectful and peaceful. This respect would derive from the understanding that one has within himself or herself that the other person is a human being also, and dealing with the world the only way he or she knows how to.

The level of fear in the African American community of those in charge of policing and keeping the community safe is at a critical point in the evolution of our country. This interaction between African Americans and police are highly likely because most Negro neighborhoods have been labeled as high crime areas and are thoroughly patrolled by police. This fear, having to potentially interact with police officials is imbedded in every African American citizen in this country. It doesn't matter where they live, what their financial status is rich or poor, or what their social status is this fear is still present. When a police car is just riding behind most African American drivers there is a level of fear that arises within the African American. This fear that arises consists of going to jail for nothing, being harassed during the stop, or even being killed during the stop takes over the thought patterns of the African American. The body's fight or flight defense kicks in when we are presented with an excessively stressful situation, such as this. We began to deplete our life force because a police car is behind us and then suddenly the police turn off on another street. We are relieved we feel we are now safe from probable harm. But unfortunately, we are unaware of what has actually happened in that moment within us. That fear has just grown stronger within us and has utilized a significant amount of our life force. This fear is so strong it has been documented that in certain incidents African American women have been stopped for traffic violations by white police and immediately begin to cry from terror. They are fearful that they may lose their lives in a simple traffic stop for speeding or a brake light not working. And the next time an incident of this nature occurs the fear will be even more intense. How can we expect to grow with such a fear imbedded in our women who care for our young?

The media also plays a role in maintaining a certain level of fear in the African American community. The media's job is to keep this fear alive through the repetitive coverage of police brutality against black. The media knows that this fear will reach more African American if properly covered and will spread like a cancer. This fear keeps the African American feeling like a second class citizen and this is the plan that is being executed at this time. These senseless killings with no prosecutions make African American feel powerless. African Americans have all the rights that any other American has but they are so distracted that they cannot grasp this concept, therefore they live in fear. And they subconsciously accept the role of a second-class citizen because of fear. We also teach our kids that if a police stop you put your hands on the steering wheel, say yes sir or yes ma'am, and do exactly what he or she says. Is this type of rhetoric, not creating fear in our youth? Why would a citizen have to worry about being killed in a simple traffic stop or interaction with police? We have to stop assuming the roles of 3/5 of a human being or the role of a second-class citizen and begin to act as first class citizens in a free world. We can never be free until we are able to resolve our fear. We must get to a point in which we are comfortable when a police car is riding behind our vehicles. We must get to a point wherein a traffic stop, we are confident in whom we are and we understand our rights. This is because fear is able to sense fear. This is also present in the animal kingdom. When you are confronted by a barking dog if he senses fear in you then he will charge, but if he senses that you will stand your ground he retreats. This is the same for interacting with humans in most cases. If you are confident in whom you are and there is no fear, then a traffic stop will be just a traffic stop. But in a traffic stop, fear appears in the form of aggressive talking, feeling the need to plead your case, or refusing commands. The vibrational frequency of fear can only remain on that frequency; therefore, the actions taken above will only have negative outcomes, thereby projecting more fear into the individual and often time into the police officer involved as well.

Once we have truly eliminated the fear of policing from our collective consciousness we can understand the universal reasoning behind the police brutality that we have witnessed the last couple of years. And that truth is that the universe refuses to allow the illusion that the world paints to lure the African American race into total sleep. Once we had witnessed the first African American president the universe understood there would be a possibility that we would be caught in the illusion that we have finally overcome. The universe knew that if the African American race felt this way that we would no longer strive for better and become the race that we are truly intended to be. Therefore the acts of police brutally would help us remain aware of the rocky road we continue to travel and help us to continue to question the state of our unity. I can recall when President Obama was elected the African American race rejoiced, and rejoiced because some felt the battle had ended. Our battle will only end when there is a total transformation of consciousness that occurs in the human race, therefore we will continue to see and battle injustices.

The universe also uses these injustices that occur to unmask those who still harbor racism in their hearts for a race of people who color is different from theirs. These people are posses by this hatred and when such hatred is present in them the light of god dims within them. If they would only examine the reason for their hate they would see an energy that is present within them that is hiding behind false concepts to continue to exist. As we continue to unify against police brutality against African Americans and we protest the social injustices that African Americans face daily, the energy of racism uses diversion techniques such as they are protesting the flag to protect its stronghold. A prime example is the protesting by NFL athletes of the social injustices African Americans face by not standing for a National Anthem that does not allow African American the rights it stands for. This reason for not standing was thoroughly explained by the players but the energy of racism turn a simple protest into the athletes are not standing for the American Flag. Therefore in the eyes of the individual that is the host of the energy of racism, it is ok to despise those African American athletes who use their stage for something greater than themselves. It is ok to say things like we can't allow the inmates to run the prison because they only understand the players united against the flag. They cannot see the energy of racism that is present within them and is controlling how they are consciously reacting to a simple cry of a people to be treated fairly under the constitution. In the eyes of these people, the athletes should be grateful for the opportunity they have to acquire money and forget about what is happening in their communities. And in these moments this is where the true growth of unity of the African American race will continue to sprout from. Because, as players begin to see the true nature of the owners of professional sports teams they themselves will unify using the money that they have acquired and being their own professional sports leagues. This has to be the next step for the African American athletes and the African American race and those who do not support racism must thoroughly support this move when it occurs. There must be an understanding amongst the African American athletes that a league does not make the stars but the stars make the league. And in all sports, the stars are primarily African Americans and this ability to become great is a part of our evolution and cannot be denied. We must understand even an inmate must one day become free, either he gains his freedom in the physical world or from death but it is gained. Therefore, our African American athletes truly have no need to run the prison, but they will one day be freed from the confines of the walls of the prison. This can only be achieved by the universal design and the most important element in that design is unity.

# Chapter 5

# Effects of Religion

The Oxford dictionary defines religion as the belief in and worship of a superhuman controlling power, especially a personal god or gods. But religion is also the signpost that points us in the direction of divinity that lies dormant within every human being. The problem occurs only when the understanding of the signpost is taken out of context or misunderstood. When this occurs we become lost, confused, and fail to find the most important thing in this world, ourselves. A person must have a high spiritual level to truly understand or teach the gospel; therefore he must be in tune with something greater than the mind but is also within him. We must understand that the people who wrote the scriptures were evolved spiritually, therefore the scriptures were written from the spirit that dwelled within them and not any forces outside of them. Also, we must understand that the mind did not create the scriptures, therefore it cannot encompass the true understanding of all the scriptures, nor can it abide by the scriptures. This is supported by Romans 8:7 which states: **Because the carnal mind is enmity against God: for it is not subject to the law of God, neither indeed can be.** When we try to understand God's laws with our thinking minds instead of feeling them in our souls, we misinterpret them and this is the current state of religion in the African American Communities. We do not truly understand what scripture is trying to teach us and these misunderstandings have held us back for generations and while continuing to prohibit our growth. We have to be honest with ourselves, our elders have been praying for change for decades with little change. People who are in need of money, healing of a sickness, the release from drug addiction, these things are rarely achieved by attending church. And we must understand why, and this understanding is critical if we expect to move our culture in a more prosperous direction. We will discuss the issues that hinder the African American community from gaining understanding and wisdom from the higher source that is in us all.

First, we must explore the actual church service to further understand what is gained by attending services. The service usually begins with praise or the singing of songs in which the main message is the hope of being saved from the world. This hope or wish for being saved by Jesus Christ from Satan, sickness or poverty has become the basis of the church experience. I once knew a woman who suffered from cancer who prayed unceasingly to Jesus, and attended church services when her health allowed her in hopes of being cured. She worked diligently in the church in between her several bouts with cancer. She could not see spending her time any other way besides attending Bible study and working in the church. Even though her life was filled with pain and the discomforts associated with cancer she persevered. She fought the disease for approximately fifteen years with the most unwavering faith in the church that I had ever seen with my own eyes. She never complained about her situation, always accepted it and continued to smile. She also had one of the most giving hearts that I have had the opportunity of experiencing in my entire life. This lady would feed the hungry, give if she had it to give, and would accept people for who they were. But even with all of her prayers, the prayers of others, and her faith in what she thought was Christianity she ended up passing away. She was only fifty- seven years of age and had been battling cancer since the age of forty-two. Upon passing away, she became a pillar of her community and in the church. I recall at her services the officiating pastor stated, "I don't understand why God takes all the good ones." At this moment, I realized that I could not be any more dedicated to the church than she was, and that I was not as giving and considerate of others as she had been. So why were the last fifteen years of her life so painful? And how many African Americans have dedicated their lives to service and experienced such a struggle? Why are so many dedicated people's life situation not being changed? At some point, we must ask ourselves how many people become truly enlightened or saved from whatever is hindering their lives by attending these church services. To become enlightened is the true goal of life and being saved by simply saying you accept Jesus Christ as your lord and savior has proven to have very little effect on the human psyche. But this has become the rite of passage of the African American churches. A man can live his life however he chooses, but when he accepts Jesus Christ all his sins are forgiven and he becomes a saved man who now has a place in the house of the Lord upon death. These are all misconceptions that hold the African Americans as prisoners to the misunderstanding of scripture and are the driving forces in our religious service. To break free of this prison we must understand who Jesus Christ was and the symbolism his name and his actions embody. The word Christ means anointed therefore it is not necessarily a name but a title according to religious scholars. But the word Christ is so much more and is truly misunderstood by the masses. The word Chris describes a state of being and is referred to as Christ consciousness. Just as Buddha describes a state of being and is referred to as the Buddha nature. The Christ is actually a shift in consciousness or the awakening of the soul by the will. Therefore when we look at the name Jesus Christ in its entirety we see that Jesus had awakened his soul which is the divine connection between man and god. In most teachings in African American churches, he is the son of God but we are all the children of God and all have infinite abilities when unlocked. This is supported by Psalms 82.6 which states, **I have said, ye are gods, and all of you are children of the most high**. The Christ dwells within each and every living human being but can only be awakened by the will of that person. So in worship, we should be seeking the Christ consciousness instead of a literal name or a man. It is the achievement of Jesus in becoming one with God that is priceless and the doorway to a higher consciousness.

**Greater is he that is in you, than he that is in the world, John** 4:4. This scripture tells us that there is a force (the Christ) that is within us that is greater than the outside world. We are not thoroughly taught the importance of this scripture. True change comes from within and not from without. This statement means that your outer world is determined by what you have within you, meaning your beliefs and thought patterns. Most churches have this paradigm backward and try to change what is within a person using forces that are outside of the body. The truth is the outer reality is ruled by the inner world and cannot be changed by words alone. The will of a man must be focused enough to cause a shift in consciousness and the awakening of the god particle (the soul) that dwells within him. If a man comes to the church for change but he has no will he will not find it in the church, the work must be done internally. This man has to first find himself and begin to truly understand who he is before any change can come. We try to skip accepting who or what we have become by attending church and repenting. This is not being authentic to the inner world therefore the outer world will not change. A man must conduct his own work within his self and use his will to force a change and not look to another person or anything external to change him. I once knew a man who was addicted to crack cocaine and had been in and out of jail the majority of his adult life. This man began to attend church in hope that he can find a way to defeat his addiction. He became saved according to the church's rite of passage and began to sing in the choir and work in the church. The church taught him by believing in Jesus he can beat his addiction but this turned out not to be the case. This man continued to use drugs secretly and eventually, his presence was not seen at any of the church services for about three months. After this three month period, he returned and began the process of trying to defeat his drug addiction again. This cycle continued for about a year and he still had not defeated the addiction. This man had not learned about the dweller within that can free him from his addiction, and was not aware that with his will he could awaken that force with him and defeat his addiction. This man continued to search externally and continued to fail. He ended up back in prison but could have avoided such a painful path if only he was properly taught. The searching for the higher self is not being taught in the African American churches and we must change that if our churches truly desire to assist in creating an empowered future for our race. We must ensure our congregations are aware of the presence within them that is infinite and eternal. They must also understand that this is our true connection to god and that this connection is the key to peace. I once knew a woman who was devoted Christian and was diagnosed with a terminal illness. This woman believed in the power of the church to heal and refused to be treated for her illness. Her children and her husband took care of her during this sickness and also hoped for a miracle cure. Unfortunately this cure did not come, and instead, death knocked on her door. She also was unaware of her inner world and that all sickness is a chemical imbalance caused by the inner world. And that her will could have awakened the Christ within her and possibly changed her situation. The church did not teach her that by just raising her self-awareness she could have possibly discovered a problem in her inner world that was causing her sickness.

There are many document cases in which an ill or individual facing an overwhelming problem is able to cause change by examining what is on the inside of them. We must understand that our emotions, thought patterns, and our beliefs are energies in the universe that our bodies respond to. A renowned author who wrote the Anatomy of the Spirit stated that our biology is our biography. This simply means our emotions, beliefs, and thoughts become the material that makes up our bodies. Therefore we must understand that when we become angry at someone or a situation that has occurred that not only are we mentally angered but every cell in our bodies become angry also. When we are jealous of another every organ in our bodies experiences this emotion. Also when we harbor or emotions or block them from manifesting on the physical plane this also has a deteriorating effect on our bodies. Our bodies are the canvases that the soul uses to paint a picture of our internal state of being. Therefore the problem is never the circumstances but always the internal state of being that is causing the circumstances. This is the soul's way of alerting the individual that they are currently in a spiritual crisis of their inner state of being is not well. And the only way to regain that balance is to look inside and discover the issues and to face them. I once read a documentary about a woman who had been in an abusive marriage in which her husband showed her very little affection. Her husband didn't respect her as a spouse or even a human being. He would abuse her both physically and mentally for the smallest things and she would take it because she thought she loved or needed him. Her husband would talk to her in the most demeaning fashion, making her feel less love than a stray dog. This lady cooked dinner every night to ensure he had food, washed his clothes to ensure he had clean work clothes available, and clean the entire house daily. She did this only to receive abuse in return. Her husband would often times cheat on her with other women and let it be known to her that he had done so and she would simply drop her head and walk into another room. She stayed with him for about five years and took this abuse day in and day out. She felt she couldn't survive without her husband even though her entire being new she needed to leave and revitalize her life into something beautiful and filled with love. One day, while bathing, she found a lump in her breast that was later diagnosed as cancer. This was her body's way of telling her that her inner world was in a crisis. She began her treatment without the presence of her husband who continued to cheat with numerous other woman and showed little regards for his action. One day her sister brought her home from a chemotherapy treatment and her husband was sitting his recliner and she asked him for a simple hug. This hug would have made her feel loved; it would have signified that he sympathized with her struggle. But instead of giving her a hug he walked out the front door and got into his car and left. In an instant, she realized that she had been giving so much of herself to this situation because she believed she needed him and this belief was destroying her body. She realized that she had lost her self-worth in him and no longer really knew herself, but only knew the pain he always made her feel. At that moment she called her sister back to the house and she found the strength and willpower to pack all her belongings and moved with her sister. She began to meditate and to examine what was inside of her, meaning her beliefs, emotions and thought patterns. This self-awareness along with her treatments helped her to rebuild a beautiful life. She had also developed the will power to change through the pain of her relationship and the sickness that was in her body. In the churches in the African American communities, we are not taught the importance of understanding the inner world and why we experience a painful situation in our lives. Granted life will never be easy because we are given this opportunity to expand the energies of our souls therefore work has to be done and we must face our fears. But regardless of what life becomes there must be an understanding that we are the creators of our circumstances and we have to accept this to transform the outer world. Scripture states that we wrestle not against flesh and blood, but against principalities, against powers, and against rulers of the darkness of this world. This scripture means that we must conquer ourselves before we can conquer the situations that we face every day in the outer world.

Our African American churches also teach our communities that we were born in sin. It also teaches us that we must repent or become saved to remove our sins. However, this too is a misinterpretation of the scripture. First, we must understand that we are tiny sparks of the infinite, which means our souls are a part of the Grand Architect of the universe and it has no sin. We are our souls, not our bodies or minds. But in the physical world the mind, body, and soul are the trinity of the physical world. This is the same as in the spiritual world the father, son and the holy spirit creates the Grand Architect's trinity. Sin comes from an untamed mind that is allowed to wonder and generate random and destructive thoughts. We must understand that we are not our thoughts and that if left untamed our thoughts can become our enemies. Thoughts possess a creative force and have the ability to manifest in the physical reality; therefore they have the ability to become a prison for the soul. Thoughts are the narrators of our reality meaning they are the voices in our heads that tell us what is going on around us. Therefore we have a tendency to think that our thoughts are who we truly are. And this misconception is very destructive and is the basis of all sin. This is because we give our power to be creators over to thoughts and the mind which both are not controlled. The outcome of this is ups and downs in life that drives us to drugs, being diagnosed with a mental illness or to attending church to find a life balance. Sadly neither drugs, whether illegal or prescription nor attending church can help a man gain control of his mind. Many people attend a two-hour church service on Sunday and during that service, the body is present but not the mind. If you ask someone who attended church service on Monday morning what did the pastor preach about he or she usually cannot recall. This is because the wondering mind was not present and this is a dangerous state to exist in. This state of being is dangerous because a man in this state is bound to sin. The narrator has the ability to make a man perceive the world through a cloudy vision which derives from that man's belief system. We then begin to judge other people and this is mostly done because the narrator or ego has something it needs to protect or sees that individual in a way that it has deemed to be negative. I once knew a young man who often times told a story about how he learned not to judge people by their appearance. He said he was walking down a busy street when bumped into a man who he thought was a racist based on his tattoos and his demeanor. The African American male said his eyes and the middle-aged white male's eyes locked on each other after the bump and they both continued on their ways. But during this brief stare-down, the young African American male had all kinds of thoughts rambling through his head. There were thoughts of calling the man a cracker, thoughts of this man hates black people, and this man has to be a member of a white supremacy group. The narrator told him just look at his haircut and the way he walks, he has to be against black people. Finally, after all of this mental chatter, the young man made it back to his car which was parked along a busy street and sat in the car for a while and continue to listen to the mental chatter. He was so engulfed in the mental dialogue that was going on in his head he forgot to look in the rearview mirror to check for oncoming traffic prior to pulling out into the busy street. The young man pulled out into the busy street and was struck by an eighteen-wheeler truck. The force of the impact broke his left arm, broke his left leg and pinned him in the car. The crushed door panel had caused a gash in his left leg that was bleeding profusely and if not stopped would have been life-threatening. The young man was in so much pain and could see his life slowly slipping from his grasp. He constantly yelled for help, but the people at the scene mostly stood around and had no idea what to do. And then out of nowhere here comes the middle age white male that he bumped into and he had accused of all type of things and called him so many names. But this man jumped right in and called 911, looked into the car and saw all the blood the young man had lost and directed others to help him free the young man from the car. The middle age man and several other people freed him from the car but by then the young man had lost so much blood he was turning pale. The middle age man began to apply direct pressure to the wound to stop the continued loss of blood. The Emergency Medical Technicians arrived on the scene and took over the care of the young black man and before they could put him in the ambulance the young man's eyes and the middle age man's eyes locked on each other again. But for the young black male this time it was different, there was no mind chatter and he saw the man in an entirely different light. He could see a man of different beliefs and emotional struggles but who in the eyes of God was still his brother. Upon arrival at the hospital the doctors told the young man another two to three minutes of blood loss and he would have not survived the incident. After the young man had fully recovered from the accident he searched and searched for the middle age man until he found him. The man's name was John and he was a former Marine who had served the country in Iraqi Freedom. He had no family and was primarily alone. The young African American male whose name was Anthony asked him to go to lunch and they ate and had a great conversation. And after three years every Friday at noon they meet for lunch and John has become Anthony's best friend. John was also Anthony's best man when he finally married his high school sweetheart. We should never judge a book by its cover and Anthony had learned this first hand. Mind chatter had caused him to judge a man not even knowing anything about this person it also had took all his focus and caused him to nearly lose his life. When a man only knows the narrator in his head he is bound to sin. In church services so many of the members are constantly judging one another, criticizing the pastors, and jealous of another's achievements. All of this comes from an uncontrolled mind. This is the true Satan that dwells in the physical world.

Also in the African American churches, we have created a being that is the opposite of God whose name is Satan. This Satan has the power that is almost equal to the Creator of all things and battles with god for the souls of men. However, this too is a misinterpretation of the symbolism in the scriptures. God is the creator of all that is and all that is not and there is nothing that exists in the physical or spiritual world that was not created by the father. Satan in the scriptures is a symbol of wrong thought. But in most churches, Satan has become an excuse for circumstances in the physical world. I once knew a woman who was very poor and lived in the heart of the ghetto. She had two small kids whom she could barely provide food for. This woman would find a job and work for approximately three months and end up being fired. She would always feel as though it was Satan causing her to lose her job. This lady would attend church services where she would receive the same message, which was Satan is the stealer of joy. This cycle continued for her, she would always lose her jobs within that three month period. She felt like she was a good employee of the companies, but Satan always made a way for her to be terminated. These constant job losses through her deeper and deeper in debt and also begin to affect her kids in a negative way. Finally, the last job she had gave her a ninety-day review of her job performance. She had received all negative marks and was underperforming in her job duties. She had been late to work three consecutive times and always returned from breaks late. She often times could not complete work assignments on time and often times needed the assistance of her coworkers to complete her job responsibilities. In that moment she realized why she had not been able to keep a job. She realized why her kids had to go without and why she lived in the heart of the ghetto. The problem wasn't a being called Satan, but wrong thought that made her feel her performance at work was acceptable. She had lost another job and went home and cried herself to sleep. She could not face her kids knowing she had not been a responsible parent and that was the cause of her life situations. After she received this awakening she went out and found her another job. And at this job she applied herself, she was always at work early and back from breaks early. She completed her work assignments before time and oftentimes was able to help others who was slower in completing the job duties. Within one month of being employed with the company she was an employee of the month and within ninety days of employment, she was promoted to a new position. After six months of employment, she was able to move her kids out of the ghetto and into a nice community. This lady had learned that wrong thought becomes the Satan that controls our lives and are often time keeps us in the situations that we are so desperately trying to improve. This is the type of understanding that has to be taught in the African American churches so that our people can begin to be responsible for their circumstances. If we continue to teach that there is a being that is responsible for all the mishaps in our lives then how many people will go through life the same way that this lady did?

**Every way of a man is right in his own eyes: but the Lord pondereth the hearts, Proverbs 21:2.** This scripture is simply stating that the father knows the true intentions behind the actions of every man. The father knows the first thought or the true thought of every prayer and this is what is answered by the heavens. The importance of knowing the intentions behind our actions is not taught to African Americans in most church service. And this is one aspect of religion that has the ability to change the lives. I once knew a woman who constantly prayed to improve her financial situation. This woman would even attend church services and ask the pastor and deacons in the church to pray for an improvement in her finances. But months passed and there was no apparent improvement in the woman's finances, in fact, it had gotten worse. She had lost her car which was her transportation to work and without transportation, she couldn't attend work; therefore, she lost her job. The woman was stuck in this financial struggle for about a year with no improvement. She didn't understand why her prayers were not answered and why was her life in such financial turmoil. It was because she was not being authentic in her prayers. The true intentions of her prayers were to gain more material wealth than her sisters. In truth, she was not in a true financial struggle but in a struggle with envy. She wanted to be on top and this was the true intention of her prayers, therefore they were not answered by the heavens. Her sisters, on the other hand, continued to prosper in their finances and receive promotions on their jobs. Often time we try to protect our true intentions by creating an intention that is more acceptable to our society. But in order to be free from the pain that we encounter in the physical world, our actions and words must be authentic to our intentions. In other words, a man must say what he means and do what he says. This is a universal law that cannot be avoided by a man lying to himself about what is truly in his heart. And the only way a man can truly change is by accepting what is truly within him and then begin to cultivate a new crop filled with new beliefs and morals.

Lastly, in the African American churches and in all other Christian churches the hope of salvation is the cornerstone of what the members are hoping to achieve. But the question must be asked, what exactly is salvation? **Restore unto me thy joy of thy salvation; and uphold me with thy free spirit, Psalms 51:12.** This scripture is stating that a man's spirit can only be saved when he becomes in control of his thought patterns. There is no other force in the universe that will come in and govern a man's thoughts; this work has to be conducted internally by the man. This is the only road to true salvation or enlightenment. This aspect of religion must be taught in order for spiritual growth to be facilitated in our churches or homes. When a man allows his thoughts to be the controller of his life, his life will only render him pain and misfortune. He will always search to conquer something new, he will always look to protect the interest of his ego at all cost, and will not hear the voice of the father in stillness. **Be still, and know that I am God: Psalms 46:10.** This stillness that this scripture speaks of can only be achieved by a man who has some control over his thought patterns. This silence is the silence of the mind, which means to cease the mind from constantly generating thoughts. And in this stillness we can find our true salvation and a place where a man can converse with the Father, and where a man can discover his higher self. I once knew a religious man who had found religion in hopes that attending church services and becoming an active member of the church will help him to cope with his problem. This man problem was he was addicted to porn and having sexual intercourse with multiple partners. He would attend church in hopes that he could find something that would help him to control his lust for sex, but often times a day later find himself looking at porn. He would try to resist these urges to engage in watching porn, but he would constantly be bombarded with thoughts and would fail to resist. This constant watching of porn would also lead him into making irresponsible decisions about his sex partners and using the proper protection when engaging in sexual acts. The cycle between attending church and losing the battle with his lust for sex continued for years to come until he became hospitalized for pneumonia. During his hospitalization, there were several tests performed and because of his reckless sexual behavior, he had contracted HIV. The man was astonished and felt like he had lost everything he had worked so hard for. As he lay in the hospital bed the man begin to cry and ask God why such a tragic thing that had occurred in his life. He had tried the only way he knew how to defeat his lust for sex and that was attending church, but it had failed to quench his uncontrollable thirst for sex. The man went into severe depression after finding out about his illness because he knew only if he had gained control he would still be healthy. This man no longer attended church services, didn't leave his house much, and refused to see any of his family members. He had become a recluse. One beautiful sunny day while sitting in his favorite recliner crying about his life, the man was attacked again by these sexual thoughts which he had no control over. He then unknowingly walked over to his desk to get on his computer to view porn, because this would satisfy these thoughts he had in his head. But this particular time was slightly different; he immediately slammed the computer to the floor and told his mind not this time. This man had realized in that moment that his mind had been controlling his sexual actions and that he was only acting a part. He then sat down and just watched the type of sexual thoughts that his mind was generating and was surprised by the content of the thoughts. In this moment he was able to realize that his thoughts were not his identity but instead, he could just monitor them and not act on the thoughts his mind manifested. This is where so many of us lose the battle .every single day. We think our thoughts are truly who we are therefore we do not seek to control them but allow them to control us. And in this paradigm, a man cannot reach salvation, but will only become a slave to the mind. And if one is a slave to the mind it will only be a matter of time before the uncontrolled mind leads them down a dark road of pain and sorrow. Therefore a man must cultivate his thoughts on what is within him. And all thoughts that will destroy, hurt, and will not facilitate spiritual growth must be discarded. We must be able to silence and control random thought in order to reach salvation. Then and only then will we be able to hear the voice of the higher self which is a divine gift to every man from our father.

We have a responsibility to our people to teach them the scriptures in the correct manner and not just from how the mind interprets the scriptures. When we teach our race incorrectly and the people being taught accepts the message to be true then they live their lives in turmoil. It takes them away from searching for the Christ within them and being responsible for their actions. It also takes them away from working towards bringing the mind, body, and spirit into harmony, therefore, raising their vibrations. And it put them in a state of being where they are not in touch with the Christ within, and they believe that Satan is the cause of all bad circumstances in their lives. Therefore they are not responsible for what is happening in their lives and therefore do not have the willpower to create change.

When we teach religion in this manner we are literally teaching people how to imprison their souls and to give up their willpower. We are all creator, whether we create consciously or unconsciously our life circumstances are ours to create and ours to change. Failure to consciously create our lives is the pain and suffering that so many of us endure.

## Chapter 6

# The Way to Liberation

In every human being, there is a battle that ensues with the energies of our souls. This battle consists of the construct of the higher and lower self or the heaven and hell allegory described in the bible. We are all fighting this battle in order to obtain inner peace, harmony, and the release from reincarnation. But so many of us are not even aware of the battle, therefore we conform to the world because this is all we know. When we allow our lower self, which consists of uncontrolled thoughts, beliefs and emotions and not the truth to be the controller of our lives we live in turmoil. The higher self consists of truth, higher states of consciousness and harmony between mind, body, and soul. When we are present as the higher self, the mind does not generate random thoughts that derive from false beliefs and is not the controlling factor of one's reality. But the mind is used as a tool to connect with the universal mind and to bring messages from the source into the physical world. The mind is also used to learn new worldly concepts, but is still a servant to the soul. It is not used to enhance the powers of the ego or to glorify the falsely created self when one is present as the higher self in this reality. The lower self uses the powers of the mind to create a self which has an ego and beliefs of how the world is or how the world should be. And this creates a false reality which pushes man away from the truth. We only begin to know the egoic self and its wants and needs, we no longer understand the needs of our soul or our true life purposes. Therefore, our souls become slaves and watch as the egoic self destroys our lives. It destroys our lives because it has an unquenchable thirst called desire, and no matter what the egoic self has accomplished in the physical world, it will always desire to have more. This thirst eats away at souls of men until there is very little left, or until the inner world is totally lost and the outer world becomes all we know. Heaven then becomes a mystical place and not a physical reality that is a depiction of our inner peace. We are now consumed by hell; our thoughts are tainted with envy, jealousy, and hate. But for every thought, every word spoken, and every action taken the law of karma awaits us. And the law of karma ensures that we are compensated for our actions both just and unjust. We then become trapped in a circle which we cannot break by conventional means; we have to awaken the higher self. But mankind has become a chaotic being who thrives on hate, violence, materialism, and strife. Collectively, we operate in the lower states of consciousness, this conclusion can be supported by the way we treat each other because of race, ethnicity, or social status. We dislike each other because of race, religious preferences, and material wealth, all of which indicate a society that operates in lower states of consciousness. If we were operating collectively in the higher states of consciousness, there would be no prisons, there would be no wars, and there would be no need for governments. But as Hermes Trismegistus said as above, so below, therefore if man has a higher and lower self then this must be true for mother earth as well. Just as our thoughts, beliefs, and actions represent our state of consciousness and until we are awakened we have very little control over them. Then we must represent the thoughts and beliefs of mother earth on a collective scale. Truly, we are made of divine energy from the source, and we are eternal beings, but we must understand that collectively we make up the construct of the world we live in. Just as our thoughts, beliefs, and emotions make up our individual worlds, everything in the universe abides by the same law. Therefore, if the collective consciousness of the human race is of the lower self then the Earth itself is also asleep and operating in the lower self. We must understand that we are a part of the earth by universal design and not because of some phenomena. We are confined to this earth in a universe that is infinite and ever expanding. We depend on mother earth for food, water, and oxygen. None of these elements have been found in outer space, we are a part of the earth, we are its thought and beliefs and we are all one. But the state of the planet is in total chaos, and the planet only knows lower states of consciousness and has not reached a state of homeostasis. There are murders by the thousands, we take from each other, there are several wars currently being fought. The rich are allowed to continue to exploit cheap labor from the poor to quench their egoic desires, but then the desires change. Children are being used as laborers in diamond and cobalt mines in Africa, and Africans in search of better lives in Europe are being misled and enslaved in Libya. Corruption and riches are all humanity knows and have become strongholds in the collective consciousness of mankind. Everyone who is asleep strives for material wealth and sometimes at the prices of the well-being of his own brother. Just as the human being who is controlled by the ego watches his life unfold unconsciously so is mother earth watching her reality unfold unconsciously. Just as in human beings there are mental constructs that represent higher states of consciousness and there are mental constructs that represent lower states of consciousness the same is true in Mother Earth. Collectively each race represents a state of consciousness for Mother Earth. This representation is reached by actions taken collectively and beliefs upheld by the majority of that race. Granted each race has people who are awake, and do not advocate violence, and their realities are not controlled by beliefs, but only by truth. But currently on earth there is a battle being waged between the higher self and the lower self. The higher self is being represented by love and peace meanwhile the lower self is being represented by vanity and war. Since the inception of civilized man, there have been races fighting to take, kill and destroy. All these acts represent a race or a group of people that operate in lower states of consciousness. There have been races or entire civilizations that sought to enslave, segregate, and destroy family structure of other human beings, and these actions are also conducive to the lower self or hell aspect in humans. Also in a human that seeks these things the light of his soul has been extinguished by his hate and greed. And there are entire races of people who came to power by using hate, by murder, and being fueled by greed. By understanding how the races in power came to be we can further understand the state of consciousness of the earth. This is because consciousness is like an empty stage and whatever it decides to allow take the stage to perform represents the true nature of that governing body and becomes its reality. And if a man watches another human being burned, hung, beaten or murdered the one who watches heart is not open but closed, and he is no longer a servant of the most high but a servant of the ego or mammon. Because if a man has not become enlighten or awaken, he will only become a pawn in the collective efforts of the lower nature of the earth to remain in control of the nature of humanity. This is where the creation of the African American race holds such value to the shift in consciousness in the world. The African American race collectively is not a race of people who set out to oppress another race by creating laws or other systems to limit rights. We are not collectively a race of violent killers as we are sometimes portrayed. What we are, is unknown to most of the world and sadly also unknown to the majority of us. But when we realize our purpose, power will be restored and our pain and suffering will not have been in vain. The African American race collectively represents an aspect of the higher states of consciousness on earth and in the human race that will soon come to power and change the world as we know it today. As mother earth begins to shift her state of consciousness from lower states to the higher states of consciousness we will see more African Americans take on higher roles in government and the decision making processes that affect our country. But before this change can occur there had to be a realization of how low the state consciousness truly was in our world. This realization is currently occurring as we speak, our government is in total chaos and the majority is dissatisfied. And this dissatisfaction and chaos clearly derive from the low level of consciousness of our elected officials, but this is in the process of changing. Soon there will be little representation in our government of the lower self, therefore laws made will reflect love and equality for all and these changes will be ushered in by the African American race and assistance from other who to are operating in higher states of consciousness. We must take into consideration that all races have individuals that have chosen to remain in lower states of consciousness and commit acts that are evil and unjust. But if we examine closely the aspects of that individual's life we can see the trials and tribulations that lead to choices he made in life. Therefore when we speak of collective consciousness we are speaking about the overall mental construct of a race. In America, we can further understand this by looking at our election process. When we are voting we primarily have two parties one that stands for sharing, helping those people in need by giving them governmental assistance and allowing people from other countries to experience the American dream. And we have another party who would like to take that assistance away, and cut taxes for the wealthy, and deny individuals from other countries the opportunity to enter America and experience the American dream. If you are not voting for sharing and assisting those in need then you are truly an aspect of the lower self in this nation., The reason for this analysis is that you clearly cannot comprehend that we are all one and if one individual suffers then we all suffer to some extent. If we closely examine the government officials elected into congress, senate, and the President of the United States we can understand that collectively we have elected officials that represent lower states of consciousness. Therefore they represent the state consciousness of the majority of Americans in the United States. They are in the process of cutting several programs that assist women and low-income families, trying to diminish the affordable health care act causing millions of people not to have health care insurance, and pushing America into another great war. All these acts do not have the aspects of love and consideration for others but instead has a vibration of greed and inequality. But on the other hand, the majority of African Americans are voting for sharing and assistance because we know someone who needs or is relying on that assistance just to eat and have a place to stay. But there are those who would rather see that person or that family hungry and out on the streets rather than to share the abundance they have accumulated. Only if they understood that the feeling of wanting another to fail or suffer has karmic reactions in the universe may be a change would occur. And this representation of higher states of consciousness by African Americans is by universal design and must be understood by the African American race in order for the world to change and liberation to begin. This is not to say one race is superior to all other races because we are all children of the Creator, but that all races must understand that the African American race represents the evolution of Earth's higher self and is about to take the stage and perform, and from this performance usher in a new reality on Earth.

In the famous words of Tupac Shakur, Born black in this white man's world, is to begin life with the weight of the world on your shoulders. You will be discriminated against and probably experience racism at some point in your life. Jobs will not come easy and almost every great achievement will be difficult to accomplish. There will also be times you may feel inferior to another race and this feeling itself may be destructive and derives mostly from the history of the race. But we must at some point ask ourselves: Why is the road travelled by the African American population so rough and rocky? Why are we looked down upon because of our skin color? We cannot find these answers in the physical world but we can find the answers if we look within ourselves. If we look deep into our being we will discover that the African

American experience is a road that can only be traveled by the strongest souls that our father has in his army. We are dominant in most sports due to our physical abilities and our mental abilities have enhanced the world's ability to communicate by the creation of the cell phone and the internet. Therefore, we must also understand that the physical world is in direct correlation to the spirit we have inside of us. In other words, if we are strong in the physical world then we must possess strong souls in the spiritual world. The definition of soul is the divine spark of light from the father that we all possess, this spark is timeless and the essence of our human experience. Therefore the sheer pain and suffering endured by the slaves were merely a testimony to the strength of their souls and where they were on their spiritual journeys. This experience can only be chosen by a soul when he is prepared to truly grow and merge with the source of the universe. I can only equate such an experience with becoming a United States Marine. Only the people who think they are strong enough to endure the torture of becoming a Marine will enlist, but only the ones who are truly prepared will emerge victorious. And when that person becomes a Marine he becomes one of the greatest warriors to ever walk the face of the earth. This is the same in the spiritual world when a soul chooses the African American experience. Only the strong will survive and upon survival, the soul is lifted to new heights in its evolution. Most African Americans are born into poverty and this is one universal design that facilitates growth in the soul. This is because a soul in poverty has a difficult time creating a strong ego, therefore it has the ability to see the world as it is and not through the eyes of his ego. I had a friend who had discovered her neighbor's children in the house all alone with no food or heat to keep them warm. She called me for assistance with the two children until social services and the police came to get the children or either their parents returned. After speaking with the children wc discovered they had been in that house alone for days and was very lucky to be found. The little boy was only 4 years of age and his name was John. The little girl was 5 years of age and her name was Anna. They both were really nice children and it truly broke my heart to see children in such a terrible situation. My eyes begin to water with tears of sorrow and I begin to question how these innocent kids ended up in such a terrible situation. About this time my friend brought them both plates of food because they hadn't eaten in days, and I watched as they begin to eat. They both smiled at each other and begin to eat off of one plate together. They were taking one bite after another smiling, laughing and enjoying the company of each other. You see when a soul is able to manifest itself as love which is the divine energy of the universe; there is no need for material wealth. I did not understand this until I was able to experience the divine love and freedom of spirit that John and Anna showed me that day. In the mist of the entire situation that they had experienced they could still smile because their hearts had not yet become cold and their minds had not yet become tamed by the world's expectations. They were still whole and still in tuned with the infinite. And this is the struggle that a soul experiences during its journey as an African American. It is how we respond to these circumstances that we face that allows our souls to pass on the next stage of evolution. This incident made me remember growing up we have very little material wealth but we were rich because we had love. The black families during this time period loved and shared with each other. Brothers and sisters' shared the last cookie, drunk from the same bottle of soda, and understood the value of loving your brother. Our grandparents played an important role in the family structure and they were more geared towards improving the next generation. And together even in such poverty-stricken times, our souls continue to expand because of love. Our ancestors who were enslaved and those that fought for civil rights understood this principle. It has been documented that while the slaves were in the fields picking cotton that they would still praise God. This praising of God was not because the slaves expected God to free them; rather it was because they understood they could not let a circumstance distance them from the father. So even when it seems like a human being should lose their will to live our ancestors still praised God. This was the universe continuing to build the foundation of the African American race. It was also documented that during the civil rights march in Selma Alabama the African Americans also were singing while being attacked by Caucasians and bitten by dogs. In all of these brutal and demeaning situations there is an element of love that vibrated from the African American soul. Even in the choosing to have nonviolent marches by Dr. Martin Luther King was a testimony to how the African American soul had evolved. Not all souls are prepared to be enslaved and beaten. Not all souls are prepared to be beaten at the hands of police, bitten by dog, or sprayed by high pressure water hoses while conducting a peaceful march. Not all souls are prepared to be transported on cramped slave ships. Not all souls are prepared to watch their parents hung, or brutally rape. Only prepared souls would choose these experiences for themselves because they understands that in experiencing these circumstances their souls will have the opportunity to expand and become closer to the source of the universe. And in knowing these truths the souls of our ancestors continued to push and never surrendered, they continued to build this elaborate foundation which could sustain the weight of the world and still smile.

The ego is defined as one's self-importance or an identity of our own construction. This self made ego is a false representation of who we truly are in this physical world. And in most cases, the African American ego is not as strong as the ego present in most other races, and this allows African Americans to accept low-level jobs with subpar pay and have some level of satisfaction with the position. And the African American ego in this weakened state also allows the living conditions to be subpar and the individual will main a level of satisfaction as well. These types of behaviors keep the individual humble and reduce the power of the ego. The growth of the soul may occur on the journey of finding financial stability in a world in which achieving such a status is difficult for the African American. If a man can gain his financial stability without compromising his core values and violating any universal laws he is on his way to achieving his spiritual goal. And because in most cases the souls that have accepted the African American experience egos are so weak they have the ability to gain their financial independence from doing what they were destined to do and not what the world or the ego wants them to become. This occurs because when a man's ego is weak he can occasionally hear the voice of the higher self. He can maintain his internal connection to the divine because his experiences of the physical world are subpar and do not possess the power to formulate a strong ego. And the individual has not yet become overtaken by the materialistic world that we live in. And even though the African American experience can be an opportunity for a soul to expand, when utilized incorrectly, it can become a weapon that has the capability to destroy a race. When we are not aware of who we truly are and the opportunity that we have, we tend to want to avoid that pain that causes us to grow.

We don't want to live in poverty so we steal, lie and cheat each other. We do not help to build up our brother, but assist in the destruction of our brother. We perceive the world only from a materialistic point of view, therefore those who possess the most riches we feel live a better life. So we begin to search for riches and this awakens the ego spirit in all men. This ego spirit destroys our ability to grow our souls and we are no longer considered to be an elite soul on a special journey. Now we eat from the same tree that all other souls eat from and that tree is called desire. Desire takes us away from our roots which is love and finding divine peace and grounds us in the lake of fire we call hell. We lose sight of our true journey and begin to create the false self. I once knew two African American brothers that grew up together in a housing project in the state of Georgia. They grew up poor and without a father. The older brother's name was James and the younger brother's name was George. The brothers together experienced many Christmas days without receiving a single gift and birthdays without receiving a simple birthday cake because their mother had a drug addiction and couldn't keep a job. They were often times picked at in school because of their clothes and also often times went to bed hungry or without adequate food. The simple things that kids needed such as love from their parents and food to eat they didn't receive on a regular basis. For the brothers, life was extremely difficult to bear, and they both found ways to cope. George the younger brother decided to cope by working harder in school. He felt that his hard work would someday pay off and his situation would be changed. James, on the other hand, comprised his core values and began to sell drugs, rob and cheat people. James felt that this road would render him nice things and put food on their table. And the selling of drugs did just that. James became one of the largest drug dealers in his city and the boys begin to dress nice every day at school. They were no longer picked on but envied by the other students. While James continued to progress down his road George remained on his course and continued to work hard in school. James could only vision having more of everything, more money, more jewelry, more clothes, and more drugs. His ego spirit had overtaken him and he was no longer in tune with the infinite. George remained humble and continued to work hard through college while his brother continued to sell drugs and run the streets. George now owns the largest law firm in his city and is a very successful lawyer while James is currently serving a life sentence in prison for murder and drug trafficking. George never comprised the energies of his soul to change his outer world; instead, he worked hard and remained humble. George understood that pain was a precursor to growth and continued to endure. James, on the other hand, comprised his true self and became a slave to the ego. James could no longer withstand the pain of the African American experience. Therefore, he changed the experience and also comprised his morals to do so. In doing so James' soul didn't expand but instead, it lost energy. We must accept the pain associated with the African American journey because life is not about the comfortable moments but it is about the uncomfortable moments that force us to challenge ourselves. Even metal must be forged in a fiery furnace and then beaten into form to become a beautiful sword that can be used in battle. This is the same with the African American experience and how it gives us an opportunity to grow if we do not lose focus on the journey. So I have to ask are you truly prepared to walk through the fiery furnace of being an African American. Can you hold on to your core values and not compromise them for material wealth? If you can stay the course you can achieve both inner and outer peace in a world filled with turmoil. **The rich man's wealth is his strong city, and as a high wall is his own conceit: Proverbs 18.11.** This scripture means that a man of wealth has a strong ego therefore has become a servant to riches. Therefore we must stay humble and continue on the quest of our souls. We must not fall a prey to the ego or we will be consumed and will never be liberated. Liberation is the key to inner peace and we are on that journey, and together with understanding of the African American experience we can achieve liberation.

Secondly, we must begin to liberate our minds meaning we must remove the deeply embedded beliefs that the world has placed upon the African American experience. All African Americans who attend public schools are taught subliminally that we are an oppressed race. We were oppressed in the past and are currently oppressed. This belief is poison to the growth and prosperity of our race. This is because we begin to act as an oppressed race and we look at our Caucasian counterparts as the oppressors, instead of looking at our thought patterns as the true culprit. The definition of oppressed is to keep a race down by severe and unjust use of authority or force. Our world appears to be oppressed because the majority of African Americans believe we are oppressed collectively, therefore the physical world mirrors the inner world. We have the power within ourselves to change this paradigm. If collectively we believe we are not oppressed and that the world is ours for the taking the physical world will follow what we truly believe. If we could understand that a soul as powerful as the souls the African Americans possess could never be oppressed by another then we become free. But to become free we must be aware of what we believe in because what we choose to believe in can become a prison for our souls. Therefore, we must understand that we are not nor can we ever be oppressed and that if we choose to collectively change this idea that dwells within the collective consciousness of the African American race then we can change it. We cannot give words, skin color, laws, and brutality the power to make us feel as though we are a second-class citizen but we must elevate our minds and in those moments understand who we are and the level of consciousness present in that person or people carrying out such an act. We must learn to see the soul of the person as our father sees such a soul. This will help us understand that we are dealing with souls that have lost their understanding of what God truly is. We must elevate ourselves above such violence and understand that there are levels of consciousness present in every human being. And when we strive to be like another race of people, accept another race's religion as ours, and look at our physical qualities as unattractive we give them the power to oppress us. When in truth, we need to look at the heart of a race and this can be examined by the actions taken collectively by that race. Therefore when you examine a race of people whose past is riddled with killing, stealing and a lack of love for the lives of others because they look different, why would you want to be like that race. This race is not a stable race collectively. This race operates in lower states of consciousness and therefore constantly creates strife and discord upon the earth's plane. Therefore we must be in tune with the nature of who we are and understand what we represent in God's army. When we look deep within ourselves we can no longer feel oppressed nor can we be oppressed by any laws or brutality that we encounter in the physical world. Because we understand that these experiences will only enhance the energies of our souls. I encounter a man named Jonathan when I was attending college who would always speak of his experiences while attending a predominantly white high school. He often spoke about how when the subject of slavery was taught in history he was often times the target of racial slurs and jokes. He discussed how notes calling him nigger or darkie was placed in his locker and how the teachers and principal both were reluctant to take actions against the other students. But he also talked about this one defining moment when the high school principal told him to get use to this type of abuse because it was the way of the world. In this moment Jonathan stated that something great awakened within him and he decided in that moment that he would not accept these actions and he would not be oppressed by others. He continued to take the abuse but held his head up high and worked hard in school. In college, he was constantly on the Dean's List and continued to push himself to greater heights. He became the CEO of a fortune 500 company and very successful in multiple business ventures. He now tells the story of the same principle which had been fired shortly after his high school graduation was applying for a job at one of his companies. And during the interview, Jonathan stated to the former principal of his high school that he was not qualified for the job he was interviewing for and that this was the way of the world so get use to it. He said the look on that principal's face was priceless. You see by changing our perceptions of certain circumstances we can grow and change our reality. And when we are capable of understanding circumstances from a deeper level oppression will no longer be a word associated with the African American experience. But will be replaced by the words endurance, perseverance, and achievement, for these are the attributes that describe who we truly are. But for such a shift in the collective consciousness of the African American race to take place we must learn to love ourselves and others, without love we will continue to journey down the road to nowhere.

Love is the fabric that holds the universe together, and it dwells within every living animal. It is a human instinct to love our children, our families, and our friends. But the love that I speak of exceeds these boundaries; it is to love men and women that we do not know that will facilitate the growth of our race. This love causes us to care for one another and want the best for each other. This love causes us to protect our neighborhoods from gangs and drugs because we want to protect the futures of the children in the neighborhoods. This love causes drug dealers not to sell drugs to their race, this love causes gang member not to kill each other. We must understand that universal love expands past our conventional boundaries, and will only make us stronger as a race. When we are unified in love we have power, real power to create change. But when we are separated and living in our own silos it is easy for another race to pick us apart. We make up only 13% of the population in the United States and when an African American is killed unjustly all 13% should demand answers. This is not to stir up racial tension but to imprint in the minds of other races that we love each other and together we shall stand. Even if standing up for our brothers and sisters cause us to lose our financial gains we must prove to ourselves and our future generations that the love for our brother is more important than the love of money. I once knew a wealthy African American man named William who had made a fortune from buying and selling real estate. He often times boasted about the influence in the Caucasian community he had because of the wealth he had acquired, and that he could no longer consider himself to be black. I couldn't understand his logic and I knew that with such an attitude that the day would come when he would realize that money is only an illusion and we must look deeper to understand the truth. His son attended an upscale private school which was primarily populated by white children whose parents were somewhat wealthy also. One day his son was called a nigger at school and had got into a fight with another white student. His son was only defending himself during the fight because the other boy had thrown the first punch. The school police who stopped the fight had pepper-sprayed William's son and slammed him to the ground. He also took him down to the police station without even asking what had happened, and allowed the Caucasian boy to return to class after initiating the entire fight. When William made it to the police station and saw his son crying and face swollen from hitting the pavement he became irate. The police had no answers, but that he had only assaulted another student. But William's son who had been reluctant to discuss the problems he had encountered at school finally told him about all the racial slurs he had endured on a daily basis trying to make him proud William was astonished. His son informed him he had been called a nigger then assaulted, and was only defending himself. His son also informed him the police asked no questions, but just sprayed him with pepper spray and slammed him to the ground. In this moment William knew that money is not the great equalizer that he had thought it was. Wealth cannot change the beliefs of another person about who you are. And during this time of need when he needed someone to keep him strong and to help him accept the pain he had to turn to the community he had chosen not to be associated with, the African American community. He received support and love from so many people until his son asked him, "Why had you turned your back on our people, why can't you accept we are African Americans?" At this moment Williams' eyes begin to tear up because he realized that money is not power but love for your brothers and sisters and investing in the future of those who support and love you is true power. You see when some of us make it or achieve what we believe to be wealth we forget about those who are not as fortunate as we are. We lose the love for our race and replace it with our love for money. But when we are faced with incidents which money has no value we tend to revert back to what is true and that is love. Love can never lose value but only increase as we multiple as a race. We must stop teaching our youth to hate each other and only come together during times of social injustices, but love each other in our everyday activities. And most of all understand who we truly are and love our brown skin for it is not a curse but a gift from the most high.

The African American race is one of the only races who have leaders that dwell on historical or past events and fail to plan for a brighter future for our race. This simply means that these leaders have not yet realized that the past is only an aspect of mind. The mind has to put events in the past, present, or future to remain organized. But the past ultimately does not exist only the present moment is where our focus truly needs to be. In other words, there is no change that can occur in past event, we can only learn from them and grow as a race. But because collectively the concentration of the African American race is on past events and achieving justice or retribution for events that no longer exist history continues to repeat itself. Our leaders are not consciously aware of this concept and continue to lead us down roads that have been travelled in the past that leads us to nowhere. In other words, it puts us in a circular motion in which we continue to repeat the past. In order to exit such a circle, we must create a clear path to where we desire to go as a race. And this path is what our leaders have failed to produce. The reason for this failure is that to create such a path one must be thinking futuristically. Our inability to be forward thinkers derived from slavery. During slavery, the majority of our ancestors' thinking patterns were consumed with wondering what the next meal would be and how to protect their families. Slavery took our ability to be forward thinkers and placed it in a bottle, therefore, containing our ability to be proactive planners. It also destroyed their ability to plan past the next day, because slaves never knew what the next day would bring therefore it was no true need for extensive planning. Meanwhile, the slave masters were creating plans to purchase more slaves, expanding their plantations, and creating laws that would hinder African American generations to come. This is the exact reason why our leaders must be capable of forward thinking and create plans that will manifest over a large period of time. Meaning it may take a couple of generations for a plan to manifest in the physical realms but without a sense of direction, we are lost. Just as when a person has no sense of direction for his life he accomplishes nothing. If we want to become a greater race of people we must establish that path and along the way have checkpoints to ensure we are heading in the right direction and not traveling in the same circle. We must plan constructively together, invest in each other futures, rely on one another's assistance, feel comforted by each other, believe together we can grow, and believe change is inevitable. What is our path and how do we ensure it is a path that is well respected by others? One thing the world understands is the ability of a race of people to generate wealth. Therefore we need to establish an organization that is backed by the African American dollar, meaning backed by our donations. Establish an organization that is backed by billions of African American dollars that is capable of backing political candidates, who is capable of purchasing the services of high profile lawyers in cases of police brutalities. A organization that is capable of using its financial wealth to correct all injustices towards the African American race. Therefore our children and our people will not get shot at traffic stops because the police will know that if they violate the rights of the individual that they will be prosecuted. They will understand the type of lawyers that will be present and the legal fight they will have to endure. But in order for such an organization to be formed, there must be a coming together for the African American people. There must be a unified front and a donation of money monthly to such a cause by all African American families and people. This will ensure that there is a future for all of our people, by investing a portion of our money back into ourselves and our communities. This is no different from the way the wealthiest organization the Roman Catholic Church remains a force in the world today. People come together and believe in the cause and donate for the continuation of the cause at hand. We must have this same attitude about the continuation and prosperity of our people. A mother should not mourn the loss of her child and because the killer was a police and the jury selected is all white the killer is freed. Leaving the mother to question the very reason why she had to be born African American. We can all come together, not just to march in the streets but to ensure that we secure the best team of lawyers and that justice is served. And in this way, the mother knows she is a part of something and that her son's death was not totally in vain. In 2016 the US Census Bureau estimated that there were 46.8 million African Americans present in the United States of America. If only half the population gave ten dollars a month to this organization just think of the wealth we can generate as a people. We can change how the entire world sees us by not living in the past but by learning from the past and planning for a bright future. This must be the path because the world only understands wealth and the ability to manipulate circumstances through wealth. But not only will we be changing our circumstances we will be shifting the future consciousness of the African American people. The young black male in school will begin to see his race as an equal and no longer as being oppressed. He will see justice being served for racial injustices, and politicians being elected who understand the African American perspectives in the United States. This is forward thinking and this is the ability to change how others view our race. Instead of being view as a race that is not unified and a race of poverty we can come together and be viewed as a race of power and financial influence. This path must be accepted by the masses and not by some in order for us to achieve success. When this path is accepted by the masses we can invest in the expansion of Black businesses, the startup of black business, invest in successful companies and continue to grow our financial influence in the world. We can establish jobs for our communities therefore driving down the African American unemployment rate. We have to believe in ourselves as a race or no one else will, it all begins and ends with us.

Lastly, to be born an African American is to be endowed with an energy that no other race present on earth has to endure and that is the energy of pain. This pain thrives in the subconscious minds of every African American and is a part of the collective consciousness of the African American experience. In our world today we are constantly being fed more energy from the media and the actions of other people around us that help this energy of pain remain a dominant power in our lives. When we see our African American athletes kneel during the national anthem because of racial inequality, and are ridiculed because they are African Americans, this act feeds our pain body. When we see police brutality against an African American citizen and no justice for the families or the individual prevails in court this act feeds the pain body. When our president makes laws that hurt the future of poor African Americans or makes derogatory comments directed towards African Americans with no repercussions this to feeds our pain body. The pain body is the aspect of our soul that consists of energy that when activated causes the mind to generate a feeling of sadness, anger, or despair. The collective pain body shared by every African America consists of our ancestors' enslavement, the feeling of inferiority, and inequality. And every time one of these three elements is activated by the conscious mind our pain bodies become stronger. In other words, every time we see a white police officer brutalize and African American and no justice is served by our judicial system we begin to experience the overwhelming feeling of inequality in America. And this single incident feeds the energy of the pain body and it distorts our perception of the world. When our black athletes are ridiculed by the president of the United States and owners of teams and other white supremacy groups for standing up for inequalities in American it makes us feel inferior as a race. This feeling of inferiority gives our conscious energies to the pain body and the stronghold of the pain body grows. When we tell our children how they should act and respect white police officers we are unknowingly awakening that pain body in them that may have been dormant. We as parents think by informing them on how to act around police we are saving the child but in truth, we are only giving life to a parasite and that parasite is the pain body of the African American experience. The pain body is a parasite and our consciousness is the host that gives it life. We must understand this is how the pain body survives, it preys on our consciousness. We must also understand how unknowingly we pass it on to the next generation, and then they will pass it on to the next. As long as there are events in the physical world that activate this pain body and forces us to pass it on to our children in hopes we are saving them the pain body survives. It attacks our race in an illusionary form and perpetuates its continued survival in the African American race. But we must also understand the laws of universal energy, and in that understanding, we can change this paradigm and become free.

The law that we must understand is the law of perpetual transmutation of energy which states that all energy in the universe is constantly moving and in and out of form. This law also relates to the energies that govern our consciousness. In other words, we can learn to harness the energies of the African American pain body and transform this energy into whatever we desire it to be. The energies associated with the African American pain body are strong and are fed almost on a daily basis, and to be capable of harnessing and transforming such energy would yield tremendous changes in our physical world.  I once knew a young boy who lived in the inner city of Atlanta Georgia who had lived in poverty along with his mother and his sister. The little boy's name was Jason and at a very young age, he began to truly dislike his family's state of poverty. He would always see the middle-class families with nice cars to drive while his family travelled on the public busing system. He would also ride by the neighborhoods in which people had nice houses and central heating and air, while he lived in the projects and only had window fans for the summer and electric heaters for the winter. Jason at a young age, vowed to move his mother out of the ghetto and into a nice home by any means necessary. In the fifth grade, Jason began to play football and discovered he was pretty good at it. He played the position of running back and one day it came to him that if he could play football good enough, he could become a professional football player and buy his mother a new home. This drive continued into high school wherein the ninth grade, he was trying out for the starting running back position for his varsity high school team and was competing for the position against juniors and seniors. Jason said during the tryout, he begin to think about how hot his home had been that summer, how his mom worked three jobs just to provide, and how he only had two pairs of jeans to wear to school. Jason unknowingly was able to harness this energy in mind. It was now Jason's time to run the ball and these thoughts continue to run through his conscious mind and at the point of receiving the ball to run he was able to transmute this energy into another form and this form gave him power and determination. Jason burst through the defensive line like a freight train and into the defensive secondary and on to score a touchdown. Jason was given the starting position for his varsity football team and continue to use the pain associated with poverty to drive him through college and on to become a star and play professional football. And finally, he realized his dream and was able to purchase his mom a beautiful home. This is an individual account of a person being able to harness energy associated with pain and transmute it into another form. Again we must understand that all energy in the universe is constantly moving in and out of form and we have the power to transform energies that govern our consciousness. In this case, he used his conscious energy to transform the energy of poverty into the energy of determination which in time generated wealth. The pain associated with growing up in poverty had driven him to success. We as the African American race have the individual responsibility to transmute the energies associated with our collective pain body into something greater. When we are faced with an incident that makes us feel inferior, we must recognize how this experience makes us feel at that moment. We must feel that energy as it takes over our consciousness and causes our emotions to boil. We must then take those boiling emotions, that painful energy and harness it, in other words, own that feeling and then transform it into your dreams and aspirations. We must understand that the collective pain body we share is not a curse but a gift and when we understand how to use it we truly become powerful. There are those people who are aware of our abilities and strive to keep us living in the illusions of inequality or inferiority. They desire to keep our pain body the controller of our lives, but as they continue to feed our pain body we must continue to transmute the energy until we are truly free. Because to be free is our birthright from our Creator which we have lost over time, but it is time to regain what is truly ours.

All that our ancestors have died for and all the inner pain we all have endured has led us to this critical point in our existence. Creation has sacrificed so many in order for the African American race to be in the place we are in this present moment. We currently have the power and now we have the knowledge to control the destiny of our race. Therefore, it is not the time to be a fretful or feel your life is ok because you have a little success, especially if behind a closed door you still harbor feelings of inferiority. It is time to be a part of the change because after reading this book you understand who you are and the universe knows about your new found understanding. You didn't pick this book up by coincidence. It is a part of the universal plan. Just as Creation can use the world's most ratcheted soil and create some of the most beautiful flowers, so has Creation used the evils that dwell in the hearts of mankind and created its new race, a race that is protected by Creation itself because it is its crowning jewel. This race is the African American race, which is a young race who is entering the peak stage of its evolution. And this peak stage will bring about great change in our nation and usher in a period of peace and love in a race that has endured the pain associated with the universal law of growth.

# References


1. Black Wall Street: The True Story. Retrieved from http://www.blackwallstreet.freeservers.com/The%20Story.htm

2. Chang'ach, J.K. (2015). If ancient Egyptians were Negros then European civilization is but a derivation of African Achievements. Retrieved from https://www.omicsonline.org/open-access/if-ancient-egyptians-were-negroes-then-european-civilization-is-but-a-derivation-of-african-achievements-2151-6200-100098.php?aid=53515

3. Emoto, M. (2005). The Hidden Messages in Water. New York, NY: Simon & Schuster.

4. Federal Bureau of Prisons. (2017). Inmate Race. Retrieved from https://www.bop.gov/about/statistics/statistics_inmate_race.jsp

5. Holy Bible: King James Version. Grand Rapids, MI: Zondervan

6.  Johnson, G.A. (2017). How do Black people spend their money. Retrieved from http://blackmeninamerica.com/updated-how-do-black-people-spend-their-money-3/

7.  Massey, M. (n.d.). Periods of Development. Retrieved from http://changingminds.org/explanations/values/values_development.htm

8.  Merriam-Webster. (2003). Merriam-Webster's Collegiate Dictionary. 11th ed. Springfield, MA: Merriam-Webster.

9.  Richardson, V. (2015). Police kill more whites than blacks but minority deaths generate more outrage. Retrieved from https://www.washingtontimes.com/news/2015/apr/21/police-kill-more-whites-than-blacks-but-minority-d/

10. The Untold Story of Emmett Louis Till. (Beaucham, K.). (2005). {DVD}. Available from https://www.amazon.com/Untold-Story-Emmett-Louis-Till/dp/B000DZ95MQ

11. US Department of Justice, Federal Bureau of Investigation, Criminal Justice Information Service Division (2013). Crime in the United States 2013. Retrieved from http://ucr.fbi.gov/crime-in-the-u.s/2012/crime-in-the-u.s.-2012/tables/43tabledatadecoverviewpdf

12. Tolle, E. (2014). When the Pain-Body Awakens. Retrieved from http://communicate.eckharttolle.com/news/2014/08/13/when-the-pain-body-awakens/